DATE DUE

GAYLORD			PRINTED IN U.S.A.

CZECH REPUBLIC
in Pictures

Stacy Taus-Bolstad

Lerner Publications Company

Contents

Website address: www.lernerbooks.com

Lerner Publications Company
A division of Lerner Publishing Group
241 First Avenue North
Minneapolis, MN 55401 U.S.A.

Library of Congress Cataloging-in-Publication Data

Taus-Bolstad, Stacy.
    Czech Republic in pictures / by Stacy Taus-Bolstad. — Rev. and expanded.
        p. cm. — (Visual geography series)
    Summary: Text and illustrations present information on the geography, history and government,
economy, people, cultural life and society of nation known as the Czech Republic.
    Includes bibliographical references and index.
    ISBN: 0-8225-4680-9 (lib. bdg. : alk. paper)
    1. Czech Republic—Pictorial works. [1. Czech Republic.] I. Title. II. Visual geography series
(Minneapolis, Minn.)
DB2013 .T38 2003   2002013954
943.71—dc21

Manufactured in the United States of America
1 2 3 4 5 6 - JR - 08 07 06 05 04 03

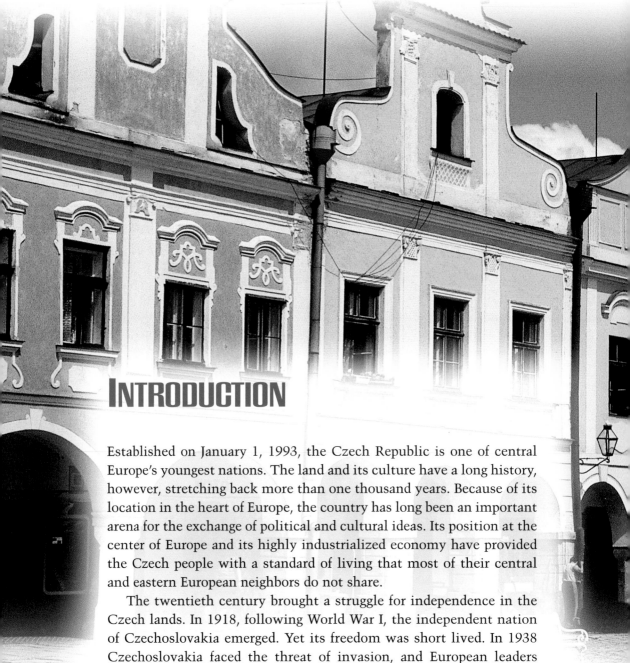

INTRODUCTION

Established on January 1, 1993, the Czech Republic is one of central Europe's youngest nations. The land and its culture have a long history, however, stretching back more than one thousand years. Because of its location in the heart of Europe, the country has long been an important arena for the exchange of political and cultural ideas. Its position at the center of Europe and its highly industrialized economy have provided the Czech people with a standard of living that most of their central and eastern European neighbors do not share.

The twentieth century brought a struggle for independence in the Czech lands. In 1918, following World War I, the independent nation of Czechoslovakia emerged. Yet its freedom was short lived. In 1938 Czechoslovakia faced the threat of invasion, and European leaders agreed to cede a large part of Czechoslovakia to Germany. Other parts of the country were given to Hungary and Poland. Czechoslovakia remained a German protectorate until the end of World War II in 1945, when it regained its freedom.

Yet the country's independence did not last. By 1946 the Communist Party of Czechoslovakia had taken control of the new government, and the country soon aligned itself with the other Communist countries of eastern Europe. The strict Communist regime imposed censorship and other restrictions on the Czech population, who lived under Communist rule for more than four decades. When mass protests forced the Communists to step down in 1989, the new nation was free to lead itself.

But the young democracy had many issues to overcome. Relations between ethnic Czechs and Slovaks soon broke down, causing a demand for an independent Slovak state. By 1992 a split was inevitable. On January 1, 1993, Czechoslovakia became two independent nations—Slovakia and the Czech Republic.

In addition to the loss of Slovakia, the new republic's ailing economy faced the challenge of moving from the Communist collective, where the state owns all industry and sets the prices of goods and

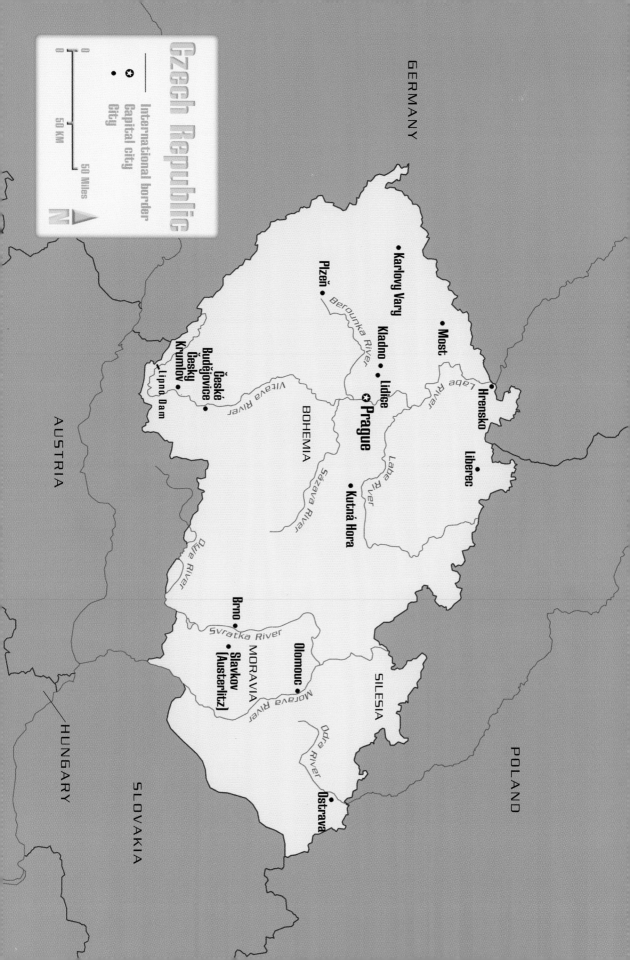

Czech Republic

International border
Capital city
City

0
0
50 KM
50 Miles

N

Karlovy Vary

Plzeň

Kladno

Lidice

Most

Hrensko

Berounka River

Labe River

Liberec

Český Krumlov

České Budějovice

Lipno Dam

Vltava River

BOHEMIA

Prague

Sázava River

Laba River

Kutná Hora

Odra River

Brno

Svratka River

MORAVIA

Olomouc

Slavkov [Austerlitz]

Morava River

SILESIA

Odra River

Ostrava

services, to a free market, where businesses are privately owned and supply and demand determine prices of products.

These changes have not come without some serious problems. The free-market system has forced unprofitable factories to close, leaving many workers unemployed. While most people are able to find jobs, prices for goods and food are rising. In addition, industrial pollution is damaging the country's air, water, and soil.

The Czech Republic made international headlines in August 2002 when devastating floodwaters covered much of the country. The floods caused damage and losses in all regions of the country, including the capital city of Prague. About 1.6 million people were affected, with more than two hundred thousand people evacuated from their homes. Cleanup may take decades, and the economic toll is estimated to be around $2 billion.

The economic woes have led to social ills, particularly crime and racism. Theft and drug-dealing are on the rise. Fear and anger over the economic situation have created religious and ethnic tensions as minorities are blamed for the nation's economic woes. Violent hate crimes present a new problem for the young government.

Despite these struggles, the young republic has emerged as a strong and independent nation. Its people are known throughout Europe as hardworking and inventive. Many foreign companies decided to invest in the country's growing economy, despite recent political turmoil. As the republic once again rebuilds, the Czechs remain steadfast in their desire to overcome past problems and to adapt to their new economy. If they succeed, the Czech Republic could become a model for the many other struggling nations in central and eastern Europe.

"I am a Czech of Slavonic blood.... That nation is a small one, it is true, but from time immemorial it has been a nation by itself and depends upon its own strength."

—František Palacký, nineteenth-century Czech nationalist

Throughout its history, the Czech Republic has experienced wars, foreign occupation, political instability, dictatorship, and economic decline. However, the Czech people have remained strong and fiercely independent. They have retained their unique national identity and continue to make important contributions to world music, literature, science, and art.

THE LAND

Located in central Europe, the Czech Republic stands at the crossroads of Europe. A small, landlocked nation, the Czech Republic is a land of mountains, forests, and lush lowlands. The country has two major regions—Bohemia in the west and Moravia in the east. The Czech Republic's neighbors are Austria to the south, Germany to the west and north, Poland to the north, and Slovakia to the east. Slovakia and the Czech Republic together made up Czechoslovakia from 1918 until 1993, when the two nations split and became independent.

Covering 30,448 square miles (78,860 square km), the Czech Republic is about the same size as the state of South Carolina. The greatest distance from north to south is about 165 miles (266 km). From west to east, the Czech Republic stretches 300 miles (483 km).

◎ Topography

Wooded hillsides, narrow valleys, and small, heavily farmed plateaus are common features of the Czech landscape. The Bohemian Basin, a

plateau that covers much of northern Bohemia, is the country's most densely populated district. This productive area has fertile farmland as well as busy industrial districts. The Vltava River and several smaller waterways wind northward through Bohemia's narrow valleys. In southern Bohemia, small artificial lakes have formed behind dams built along the rivers.

Mountains and uplands surround the Bohemian Basin. The Ore Mountains—known to Czechs as the Krusne Hory range—form a natural boundary in the northwest with Germany. The taller Krkonoše Mountains are part of the Sudeten Range and border Poland in the northeast. This range includes Mount Sněžka (5,256 feet above sea level; 1,602 meters), the highest point in the Czech Republic.

In southwestern Bohemia are the Český Les and Šumava ranges, both part of the Bohemian Forest. This sparsely populated area has a harsh climate and thick woodlands. To the east of this region, the Bohemian-Moravian Highlands stretch across the Czech Republic

SILESIA

In addition to Bohemia and Moravia, the Czech Republic has a third historical region—Silesia. The tiny area, which sits between the Czech Republic and Poland, contains rich coal reserves. Factories fueled by coal spew black smoke over part of the region, giving Silesia the nickname the Black Country.

Factories in the small region of Silesia belch smoke into the area's atmosphere.

from central Bohemia into Moravia. Small towns and lakes dot the green hills of these highlands, which are crisscrossed by rivers and streams.

A mostly agricultural region, Moravia is divided into North and South Moravia by the Morava River. In the river's valley are industrial cities, mining centers, rural villages, and farms. West of the valley are the plains and low hills of the Moravian Lowlands. The Morava and other rivers of this area flow southward toward the Danube River, one of Europe's longest and busiest waterways.

The Jeseník Mountains rise in northern Moravia near the border with Poland. South of the Jeseník Mountains is an area of harder limestone rock known as the Moravsky Kras, where water erosion has formed caverns, underground streams, and strange rock formations. To the east lie the foothills of the Carpathian Mountains, which cross Slovakia.

◉ Rivers

The landlocked Czech Republic has links to other nations through its principal waterways. Most of these rivers have not become major shipping routes, however, because the Czech Republic lies far from any major ports. Riverboats carry only about 5 percent of the nation's cargo, and most Czech goods still travel by road or rail.

The Labe River begins in the Krkonoše Mountains and then flows southward into the fertile lands of the Bohemian Basin. The river

A fisher tries his luck in the **Vltava River** near central Prague.

curves to the west and north before entering a narrow valley in the Ore Mountains. After crossing the German border, the Labe becomes the Elbe and eventually reaches the North Sea, part of the Atlantic Ocean.

The Vltava River starts in a remote section of the Bohemian Forest. After leaving these highlands, the river turns sharply northward and cuts a narrow valley through southern Bohemia. Several smaller rivers, including the Sazava and Berounka, rush down from the surrounding highlands to join the Vltava.

The Vltava passes through Prague, the capital of the Czech Republic, before emptying into the Labe River. Barges and some passenger ships travel on the waterway. The Czech government plans to deepen the river's channel to improve it as a transportation route.

The Morava River flows from north to south through a densely populated valley in Moravia. The Odra, a mountain river in the northeast, traces a northward course into Poland. The Dyje and Svratka Rivers join in southern Moravia and eventually reach the Morava, which in turn empties into the Danube.

◉ Climate

The Czech Republic has a variable climate, which means altitude affects both temperature and precipitation. Summers are warm, with frequent thunderstorms. Prague's average temperature in July, the warmest month, is 67°F (19°C). The country's summer temperatures vary between 73°F (23°C) and 84°F (29°C) depending on elevation.

Blanketed by snow about six months of the year, the **Krkonoše Mountains,** or Giant Mountains, are a popular destination for skiers.

Winters in the Czech Republic are long, cold, and usually dry. Many days are cloudy, with light snow and rain. Prague averages 29°F (–1.7°C) in January, the coldest month. Moravian cities are usually colder. Snow covers the mountains of the Czech Republic from November to April, but people living in the lowlands rarely see heavy snowfalls.

Throughout the year, temperatures are cooler in the highland regions. Winds from the Atlantic Ocean to the west and the Adriatic Sea to the south bring more than 40 inches (102 centimeters) of annual rainfall to the mountains of Bohemia. But these ranges also block precipitation at lower elevations. As a result, the plains and valleys of the Czech Republic get less than 21 inches (53 cm) of rain and snow during the average year.

Flora and Fauna

Dense forests, mainly in mountainous areas, cover about one-third of the Czech Republic. But more than half of the nation's land has been cleared for farming and industry. Acid rain (rain tainted by pollution from heavy industries) has also destroyed large forests in Bohemia, especially in the Ore Mountains.

Coniferous (evergreen) trees, such as spruce and fir, thrive in the highlands at higher elevations. Deciduous (leaf-shedding) trees such as beeches are common in the hills of Bohemia and Moravia, and oak forests line the valleys of the Labe and Morava Rivers. Many Czech lowlands have mixed forests of ash, beech, maple, oak, and spruce trees. Wild grasses, clover, and reeds are common along the riverbanks.

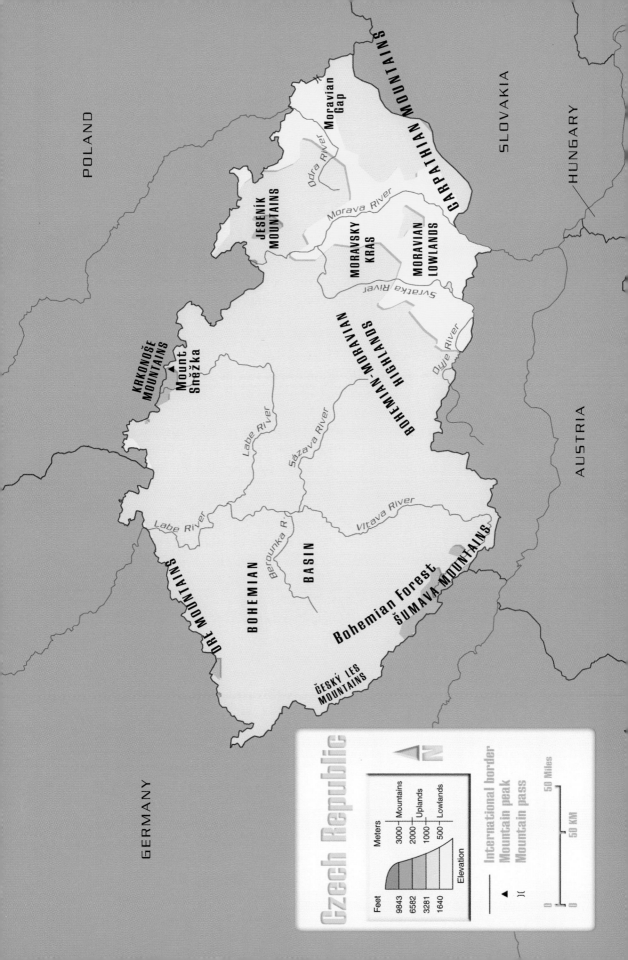

POLAND

SLOVAKIA

HUNGARY

GERMANY

AUSTRIA

Moravian
Gap

Odra River

Morava River

JESENÍK
MOUNTAINS

CARPATHIAN MOUNTAINS

MORAVSKY
KRAS

MORAVIAN
LOWLANDS

Svratka River

Dyje River

KRKONOŠE
MOUNTAINS

Mount
Sněžka

BOHEMIAN-MORAVIAN
HIGHLANDS

Labe River

Sázava River

Vltava River

BOHEMIAN
BASIN

Berounka R.

Labe River

ORE MOUNTAINS

Bohemian Forest
ŠUMAVA MOUNTAINS

ČESKÝ LES
MOUNTAINS

Czech Republic

N

International border
Mountain peak
Mountain pass

Meters		Feet
3000 — Mountains		9843
2000 — Uplands		6582
1000 — Lowlands		3281
500		1640

Elevation

0   50 KM   50 Miles

Deer, foxes, wolves, lynx, martens, minks, and chamois (mountain antelope) live in the remote mountains and forests of the Czech Republic, which are also home to the mouflon, a mountain sheep. Hare and badgers inhabit the lowlands. Common birds include wild geese, partridges, pheasants, and wild ducks.

Natural Resources

Fertile soil, the country's most valuable natural resource, has allowed the Czechs to become self-sufficient in food production. The country's mineral resources include coal, a fuel source that is abundant in northern Moravia, in the valley of the Odra River, and near the city of Plzeň in western Bohemia. The Ore Mountains have large deposits of lignite, or brown coal, which is burned to generate electricity.

Workers in the Czech Republic also mine lead and zinc. Iron ore and magnesite provide raw materials needed by the steel industry. Supplies of uranium ore fuel the nation's nuclear power plants. The largest deposits of these minerals are found in the Ore Mountains.

The Czech Republic has fields of oil and natural gas, but the reserves are too small to meet the growing demand for gasoline and for fuel to heat homes. The rapids of the Vltava River power several hydroelectric plants, which convert the energy of flowing water into electricity.

Cities

During the nineteenth century, industrialization and the spread of railroads helped the country's cities grow rapidly. In modern times, 77 percent of the nation's 10.3 million citizens live in urban areas. The largest cities, such as Prague and Brno, are located near major rivers. The mountainous regions of Bohemia and Moravia are home to small towns and villages.

A bustling city of 1.2 million people, Prague (called Praha in the Czech language) lies along the hills and bluffs of the Vltava River Valley in north central Bohemia. The historic capital of Bohemia, Prague has become the economic and political center of the Czech Republic, as well as an important cultural hub of central Europe.

Commonly known by the Czechs as Zlatá Praha, or Golden Prague, the Czech

Prague is often called Zlatá Praha, or Golden Prague. While no one knows the true origin of this nickname, myths and legends abound. One popular legend claims that the name goes back to the 1500s when alchemists—scientists who tried to turn metals into gold—made Prague their home base.

Located at the heart of Prague, **Old Town Square** is home to municipal buildings, medieval homes, and sidewalk cafés. To find out more about Prague, go to vgsbooks.com.

Republic's capital city has a long and colorful history. After the city's founding in the ninth century A.D., Prague became the seat of Bohemia's kings. In the 1300s, Emperor Charles IV of the Holy Roman Empire built new palaces, churches, bridges, and a neighborhood known as Nove Mesto (meaning "new town" in the Czech language). In 1918 Prague became the capital of the new Republic of Czechoslovakia.

Despite the two world wars fought across Europe during the twentieth century, Prague escaped aerial bombing and heavy damage. Much of the historic center, including Nove Mesto and Stare Mesto (Old Town), survived. However, in 2002 floodwaters covered most of the city, damaging many of the city's historical treasures and forcing many people out of their homes.

Brno (pronounced BUHR-naw), the Czech Republic's second largest city, has a population of 387,000. Located in southern Moravia, Brno is an industrial hub that produces motorcycles, textiles, and heavy machinery. Founded one thousand years ago, it served as the capital of Moravia when the region was part of the Hapsburg Empire. It later served as headquarters for French emperor Napoleon Bonaparte in the

Spilberk Castle *(left, on hill)* overlooks Brno. Built as a home for royalty in the thirteenth century, it became a museum dedicated to Brno in 1960.

1800s. One of Brno's major attractions, Spilberk Castle, was the site of a notorious prison and torture chamber under Hapsburg—and later, Nazi—control.

The Czech Republic's third largest city, Ostrava (population 324,000), lies near the Moravian Gate, a mountain pass that links Poland and Moravia. Many of Ostrava's citizens are of Polish descent, and the city has close cultural and economic ties to Poland. Factories in Ostrava produce iron and steel, machinery, and chemicals. These businesses employ thousands of workers, but they have also caused severe air pollution. As a result, Ostrava is one of the unhealthiest urban centers in the Czech Republic.

Plzeň (population 175,000), a city in western Bohemia, was founded by King Wenceslas II in 1290. Although most famous for its Pilsner beer, Plzeň has also been a center of weapons production. The huge Skoda factory, for example, once made armaments as well as aircraft, heavy machinery, railroad cars, and textiles. The city also has an important college of engineering that prepares its students for careers in industry.

Environmental Issues

The Czech Republic's industrialization has helped its people maintain a high standard of living for more than a century. But the country's industry has also extracted a high cost. Parts of the Czech Republic are some of the most polluted areas in the world.

Toxic fumes from factories and exhaust from old cars darken the skies of many Czech cities, particularly Prague. People in the capital city are advised to remain in their homes when air pollution reaches high levels. Villages and towns dump waste into the many rivers and streams that flow through the country, polluting the important water supply for animals and humans alike. Acid rain takes its toll on the countryside, affecting almost 60 percent of the country's forests.

The government is working to reduce these environmental hazards through public awareness and newer, cleaner sources of energy. Nuclear power plants hope to provide about half of the country's fuel needs. Homeowners are encouraged to switch from coal to natural gas, a cleaner fuel source. While these cleaner burning fuels will reduce the Czech Republic's air pollution, they present their own problems. Natural gas mining operations and toxic waste from power plants raise new environmental issues that the country will have to address. Until solving environmental issues becomes a high national priority, pollution will remain an ongoing problem.

These **Norway spruce trees** in a forest near the town of Hora Svateho have been destroyed by acid rain.

HISTORY AND GOVERNMENT

The area that makes up the modern Czech Republic has been inhabited since ancient times, when cave dwellers lived in the region's mountains and valleys. By 4000 B.C., a group of unknown origin settled in the area that later became Prague.

The Boii, a Celtic people from northern and eastern Europe, settled in Bohemia in the second century B.C. and gave the region its name. Their villages and their largest city, Boiohemum, prospered from trade.

The Boii soon faced invasions by the Teutons, a nomadic group that settled in lands to the west. Bohemia and Moravia faced turbulence in the first century A.D. as nomadic invaders and Roman forces, based in what became Italy, clashed over land and trade. At its peak, the Roman Empire covered western and central Europe, extending as far north as Great Britain and west to Portugal. It also stretched east into Turkey and south into Egypt.

By the fourth century A.D., the Roman Empire split into western and eastern halves. This division had a great impact on the peoples of central

Europe. After the split, Constantinople (modern Istanbul, Turkey) became the capital of the Eastern Roman, or Byzantine, Empire. Rome remained the principal city of the Western Roman Empire. Both of these cities were important centers of Christianity, a Middle Eastern faith that the Roman Empire had adopted as its official religion.

In the A.D. 400s, Teutonic groups pushed into southern Europe and Italy, and the Western Roman Empire collapsed. After the Teutonic invasions, huge numbers of Slavs began moving into central Europe. The largest group of Slavs to arrive in Bohemia during this "Great Migration" were the Cechove, or Czechs.

The Slavs divided into eastern, southern, and western groups. The eastern Slavs settled in Russia, while the southern Slavs moved into the Balkan Peninsula of southeastern Europe. The western Slavs built their villages in the plains and river valleys of north central Europe. Western Slavs made up the largest ethnic group in Poland, Bohemia, Moravia, and Slovakia.

Charlemagne, a brilliant military leader, created an empire that stretched from the Atlantic Ocean east to what later became the Czech Republic. Visit vgsbooks.com for links to websites where you can learn more about the history of the Czech Republic.

Foreign Occupation

Around A.D. 500, the Slavs suffered a devastating invasion by the Avars, who came from central Asia. The Avars ruled Bohemia until a German tribal chief named Samo arrived in the early seventh century. In 620 Samo allied with the Czechs, defeated the Avars, and established a new state under his rule in 623. Bohemia remained independent until 658—the year of Samo's death.

After Samo's death, the Czechs faced a new threat from the west—the Franks. By 805 Bohemia and Moravia were paying tribute (money) to the Frankish ruler Charlemagne, who made these regions into frontier provinces of his realm.

Charlemagne united much of western and northern Europe into the Frankish Empire. Closely allied with the Roman Catholic Church, the Franks forcibly converted many Slavic groups to Christianity.

After Charlemagne's death in 814, the Frankish Empire was divided among his descendants. These states, which would later become Germany, would often play a role in the affairs of the Czechs in the coming centuries.

In 833 a Slavic chief named Mojmir founded the Great Moravian Empire, a state that included parts of Bohemia, Moravia, Poland, and Slovakia. Under Mojmir and his successor, Rastislav, Moravia formed closer ties to the Byzantine Empire. Although Mojmir and other Slavic leaders had accepted the Roman Catholic faith, Rastislav invited missionaries into Moravia.

In 894 the Magyars of central Asia invaded Europe. The powerful Magyar cavalry destroyed the Great Moravian Empire. After establishing the Kingdom of Hungary to the southeast, the Magyars occupied the area of Slovakia for nearly one thousand years.

At the same time, the Přemyslids—a group of Czech princes—extended their rule over Bohemia. One of these leaders, Prince Wenceslas, swore allegiance to the German king. This action roused the anger of Bohemia's princes, and Boleslav, the brother of Wenceslas, murdered him in 929. Boleslav then became the second ruler of the Přemyslid dynasty (family of rulers).

The members of the Přemyslid dynasty often quarreled among themselves over who would succeed to the throne. This political instability soon took its toll. By 950 the German ruler Otto I made Bohemia part of the Holy Roman Empire. This huge state included hundreds of cities and kingdoms in central and eastern Europe. Because Otto I was closely allied to the Catholic pope in Rome, he was given the title of emperor. Bohemia became a fief—a state that paid tribute to the Holy Roman emperor. Despite being part of the Holy Roman Empire, Bohemia's kings were largely allowed to govern the region.

LIBUSSA

Many nations have legendary origins, often blending history with myth. The Czech Republic has Libussa, the fabled mother of Bohemia. A wise princess who may have been the granddaughter or great-granddaughter of Samo (the Czech leader who established the first western Slavic state), Libussa became leader of the Czechs after her father died.

When an elder of the tribe expressed disgust at being ruled by a woman, Libussa retorted, "You need a ruler more severe than a woman, and you shall have him." She sent out messengers with instructions to find Přemysl, a plowman from a neighboring hamlet. When they returned, Libussa married Přemysl, and together they founded the Přemyslid dynasty.

End of the Přemyslids

In 1034 a Přemyslid prince named Bretislav became King of Bohemia. Bretislav hoped to foster ties with the German king and encouraged Germans to immigrate into the kingdom. The German immigrants founded settlements throughout western and northern Bohemia. The kingdom adopted a German code of law and carried on much of its trade with German cities. The Holy Roman emperors sent German clergy into Bohemia to strengthen German influence, which would remain an important factor in Bohemia's history.

King Otakar II expanded the kingdom by gaining extensive lands in Austria through military conquest and a marriage alliance. Otakar II died in 1278 while fighting Rudolf II, an Austrian noble. After this battle, Rudolf founded the Hapsburg dynasty, which would become the ruling house of the Holy Roman Empire.

The Přemyslid dynasty ended when Wenceslas III died in 1306 with no successor. John of Luxembourg, a foreign king who married a Přemyslid princess, claimed the throne of Bohemia in 1310. Not all Bohemians accepted John as their monarch, however. For many years, the kingdom suffered civil war as the nobles fought with John and with one another for power.

The reign of John's eldest son, Charles IV, was known in Bohemia as the Golden Age. Charles strengthened the royal administration and added several fiefs to the kingdom. In 1355 he also became the Holy Roman emperor.

Under the leadership of **King Charles IV,** Bohemia became one of the most powerful states in central Europe.

Symbolizing the struggle of the Czech people, a **statue of Jan Hus** stands in Prague's Old Town Square. It was erected in 1915, five hundred years after Hus was burned at the stake.

Charles transformed Prague into an imperial capital by raising new buildings, churches, and monuments. He refurbished Prague Castle—the ancient seat of Bohemia's kings—and made the city into a center of learning by founding the University of Prague in 1348.

The Hussite Wars

In the mid-1300s, Bohemia's religious leaders questioned the power and vast wealth of the Catholic Church and the popes who ruled it. Many of Bohemia's Catholic priests joined a movement for religious reform. Although many Czechs supported these priests, most Germans in Bohemia remained loyal to the pope.

After the death of Charles IV in 1378, religious clashes broke out between Czechs and Germans. In 1411 Jan Hus, the head of the University of Prague, rebelled against the pope's authority. Hus quickly gained a wide following among the Czechs, who saw him as an important symbol of independence from the Holy Roman Empire and from German authority. But in 1415, Catholic leaders condemned Hus and he was burned at the stake.

The execution touched off decades of religious and ethnic warfare in Bohemia. German Catholics and Czech Hussites (supporters of Jan Hus) clashed in Prague and other cities. Jan Žižka, a Czech noble, led an army of Hussites that looted German towns and destroyed Catholic churches. Žižka's campaigns forced many ethnic Germans to flee Bohemia. To retaliate, the pope called for a religious war against Bohemia.

As battles raged in Bohemia, the realm was without a king. In 1458 the Bohemians elected George of Podebrady, a Hussite, as their king. But the pope and many Catholics opposed this ruler, who died without a successor in 1471. For years afterward, the Czechs formed rival camps and fought in support of their favorite candidates.

The Bohemian nobility took advantage of these conflicts to increase their power over the kingdom's townspeople and peasants. In 1487 the nobles established serfdom on their estates. Under this system, Czech peasants were bound to the estates as the legal property of the landowners.

Hapsburg Rule

The religious and civil conflicts weakened Bohemia during the time of a serious foreign threat. In the early 1500s, an army of Ottoman Turks invaded central Europe from their bases in Asia Minor (modern Turkey). To prevent Bohemia's conquest by the Ottoman army, the Czech parliament allied with the powerful Hapsburgs of Austria and accepted a Hapsburg prince, Ferdinand, as the new king.

Meanwhile, another religious rebellion was brewing in Wittenberg, Germany, where the priest Martin Luther was protesting corrupt practices of the Roman Catholic Church. Luther and his followers—known as Protestants—founded an independent church. Both Czechs and Germans in Bohemia joined Luther's call for reforms, known as

In 1521, after he publicly critcized the pope and Church practices, German priest **Martin Luther** was expelled from the Roman Catholic Church.

The **Defenestration of Prague** set off the Thirty Years' War. In 1618 Czech nobles defenestrated Hapsburg advisers, or threw them out a window.

the Protestant Reformation, and the Czechs founded a Protestant church in Bohemia.

The Hapsburg dynasty was loyal to the Catholic Church and opposed to the Protestant Reformation. In 1547, after Ferdinand put down a rebellion by Czech Protestants, the Hapsburg ruler declared Bohemia to be a Hapsburg territory. Too weak to resist the Hapsburg decree, Bohemia and Moravia would remain part of the Hapsburg Empire until the twentieth century.

In 1617 Ferdinand II, a staunch ally of the Catholic Church, inherited the Hapsburg throne. Ferdinand was determined to stamp out Protestantism in the territories under his control. In 1618 a group of Czech nobles protested this policy by throwing three of Ferdinand's advisers out of a window of the Prague Castle.

The advisers survived, but the Czechs were forced into open rebellion, sparking the Thirty Years' War between European Catholics and Protestants. The parliament elected a Protestant to rule Bohemia and enlisted an army to fight the Hapsburgs.

In November 1620, the Hapsburgs crushed Czech forces at the Battle of White Mountain. After the battle, the Hapsburg armies drove rebellious Czech nobles out of Bohemia. Czechs who remained lost their independence, including individual rights, property, and religious freedom. Ferdinand also stripped the Bohemian parliament of its power to make and enforce laws.

In 1648 the Treaty of Westphalia ended the war. By the terms of the treaty, Bohemia and Moravia remained Hapsburg territories. Czech Protestants who had not died in battle were forced to leave the kingdom. The Hapsburgs prohibited teaching and publishing in the Czech language, and German became the official language of government and education.

Maria Theresa's Reign

Maria Theresa became the Hapsburg empress in 1740. The new empress drew Austria and Bohemia closer together and created a more efficient government. Under Maria Theresa's more liberal regime, Catholic control lessened and Czech culture began to revive.

Members of the Bohemian nobility started new industries, such as textile mills, glass factories, and coal mines. Bohemia, Austria, and Moravia formed a new customs union that helped trade among these regions and improved their economies. Bohemia soon became the most industrialized area of the entire Hapsburg Empire.

Joseph II, who succeeded Maria Theresa in 1780, made further reforms in the Hapsburg Empire. He granted complete freedom of

Shown here with her family, **Maria Theresa** *(seated at right)* abolished the separate administration that the Hapsburgs had used to govern Bohemia.

Hapsburg ruler **Francis II** *(left)* **meets with Napoleon** *(right)* after the defeat of the Hapsburgs at Austerlitz in December 1805.

worship to Protestants, wrote a new code of laws, and allowed the Czechs to publish a newspaper in the Czech language. Joseph also abolished serfdom throughout the realm. For the first time since the late fifteenth century, Czech peasants were free to leave their homes and farms. Bohemian and Moravian cities grew rapidly as new factory jobs attracted these farmers to the cities.

At the end of the eighteenth century, French general Napoleon Bonaparte invaded Germany and Austria. Napoleon defeated Hapsburg forces at the Battle of Austerlitz in southern Moravia in 1805. This clash brought about the collapse of the Holy Roman Empire in 1806. The Hapsburg ruler Francis II became the head of a new Austrian Empire, which included Austria, Bohemia, Moravia, Hungary, and parts of Poland and Italy.

National Revival and the Czechoslovak Republic

By the 1840s, Czech leaders demanded political reform and an end to German influence. Historian František Palacký wrote the *History of Bohemia*, a book that revived interest in Czech history and culture. State schools began teaching the Czech language, and writers used it in their works.

In 1848 open revolt against monarchic rule broke out in several European capitals, including Prague and Vienna. Hapsburg forces put down the rebellion in Prague and installed strict martial rule over Bohemia and Moravia. In the 1860s, these regions became part of Austria-Hungary, a dual monarchy that replaced the old Austrian Empire.

Throughout the late 1800s, the long-standing conflict between Czechs and Germans in Bohemia worsened. While Czech nationalists attempted to win more freedom, German and Hungarian politicians in the Austrian parliament stopped the effort. The government, however, did begin writing laws for Bohemia and Moravia in the Czech language.

The Czechs were one of many peoples to demand independence from Hapsburg rule in the early twentieth century. The decline of the Ottoman Empire, which had ruled the Balkan Peninsula for centuries, also sparked revolt in southeastern Europe. As these challenges to Austrian and Turkish power grew, rival nations, including the Russian Empire, moved into central Europe to claim territory and influence.

These conflicts led to the outbreak of World War I (1914–1918). Austria fought the Serbs, one of the Slavic peoples seeking independence from Hapsburg rule in the Balkans. In alliance with Germany, Austria also battled Russia in the east and Italy in the south. The Czechs, however, had little desire to fight against the Serbs and Russians, their fellow Slavs. Many Czechs fled to Russia to join a force made up of Czechs and Slovaks.

During the war, Czech leaders Tomáš Masaryk and Eduard Beneš and the Slovak politician Milan Stefanik planned for an independent nation of Czechs and Slovaks. Masaryk promised the Slovaks a separate government within this postwar state. On October 18, 1918, as Germany and Austria suffered defeat on the battlefield, Masaryk declared the independence of a new Czechoslovak nation. Ten days later, Czechoslovakia was established, with Masaryk as its first president.

Accompanied by soldiers, **Czech president Masaryk** *(center, in top hat)* returns to Prague after World War I. He spent the war years abroad gaining support for independence for Czechoslovakia.

Freedom Won and Lost

The borders of Czechoslovakia encompassed Bohemia, Moravia, Slovakia, and Ruthenia, a small region lying east of Slovakia. Several ethnic minorities lived within these borders, including Germans in the west and Hungarians in the southeast.

In 1920 the Czechoslovak legislature passed a democratic constitution that established the bicameral (two-chamber) National Assembly. Despite Masaryk's promises to the Slovaks, no separate administration was created for Slovakia. Ethnic Czechs dominated the Czechoslovak legislature and judicial system.

Although the economy of Czechoslovakia benefited from new postwar industries, conflict among Czechoslovakia's many ethnic groups continued. Slovaks wanted self-rule, while Ruthenians and Hungarians felt little loyalty to the central government. Ethnic Germans living in the Sudetenland in northern and western Czechoslovakia sought closer ties to Germany.

Germans had little representation in the Czechoslovak legislature, however, and the nation's high taxes fell heaviest on wealthy German citizens. A program of land reform allowed the government to seize German estates, which were then turned over to Czech peasants. The government also resettled ethnic Czechs in German-speaking regions. Although many Germans supported the government, others strongly opposed these measures and sought to unite the Sudetenland with Germany.

When Adolf Hitler and the Nazi party took control of Germany in 1933, many Sudeten Germans allied themselves with Hitler, who threatened to take over the Sudetenland. Hitler vowed to establish an ethnic German empire in Europe.

In 1938 Britain, Italy, and France made a treaty with Hitler to avoid another world war. Called the Munich Agreement, the treaty allowed Germany to occupy all Czech territories in which more than half the population was German.

As a result, Germany received 38 percent of Czechoslovakia's land and ruled 2.8 million Sudeten Germans and 750,000 Czechs. The German government also forced Eduard Beneš—who had succeeded Masaryk as president in 1935—to resign. Emil Hácha, who accepted many German demands, took the presidency.

Hitler still sought to occupy the rest of Czechoslovakia, whose weapons factories

Eduard Beneš

Czechoslovaks look on as **Nazi troops roll into Prague** on March 15, 1939.

would help Germany's military. To avoid further conflict with Germany, Hácha's government agreed to grant independence to Slovakia and Ruthenia. Nevertheless, Hitler ordered an occupation of Bohemia and Moravia in March 1939. The small Czechoslovak army offered no resistance, and German troops quickly marched into Prague. Germany took control of Czechoslovak industries, and Bohemia and Moravia became a part of the Nazi empire.

Germany's invasion of Poland in September 1939 touched off World War II. France, Britain, the United States, and the Soviet Union fought Germany, Italy, and Japan. In Czechoslovakia millions of workers and students were forced to labor in factories to supply armaments for the German military. Opponents of the Nazis and nearly 100,000 Czech Jews were arrested and sent to concentration camps, where most were killed.

Because Germany had already occupied most of Czechoslovakia, however, Czech cities suffered less fighting, bombing, and damage than other cities in central Europe.

Eduard Beneš, who had fled to Britain, established a provisional Czechoslovak government in London during the war. Beneš also signed a treaty of friendship with the Soviet Union.

While European Jews made up the largest group of people persecuted by Hitler's regime, they weren't the only group sent to Nazi concentration camps. During World War II, anywhere from 250,000 to 500,000 Roma, (Gypsies), including those living in Czechoslovakia, were systematically deported to the camps. The Romany word for the camps, *porajmos*, means "devouring."

Czechoslovak fighters fire at Nazis from behind makeshift barricades in May 1945. This revolt is known as **the Prague Uprising.**

Meanwhile, Czechoslovak political parties formed guerrilla groups to fight against the Nazi occupation. One of these groups, the Communist Party of Czechoslovakia (CPCz), organized a resistance movement from the Soviet capital of Moscow.

In the fall of 1944, the Czechoslovak guerrillas took advantage of German defeats in eastern Europe to step up fighting in Czechoslovakia. In May 1945, a full-scale revolt broke out in Prague. When Germany surrendered on May 7, Soviet troops and Czechoslovak guerrillas took control of Prague, while U.S. armies occupied southern Bohemia.

After the war ended, the United States, Britain, and the Soviet Union met to decide the future of central Europe. The three nations agreed to revive the Czechoslovak state and to expel most Sudeten Germans from the country. The Czechoslovak government, under Eduard Beneš, allied with the Soviet Union.

Communism

The Czechoslovak Communist Party won a majority of votes in the first postwar elections. For three years, the Communists shared power with other parties in a coalition government, with Beneš serving as president. Favoring state control of the economy, the Communists put many Czechoslovak industries under government ownership.

The growing power of the Communists alarmed many of their

A crowd gathered in Prague in February 1948 to demand a Communist government. Some waved Soviet flags to show their support for the Communist Party.

opponents in the government. In early 1948, the Communist Party staged violent rallies in Prague. To avoid further turmoil, Beneš appointed a new government dominated by Communist leaders.

In 1948 Klement Gottwald of the Communist Party replaced Beneš as president. Gottwald's government banned opposition parties, turning Czechoslovakia into a strict one-party state. The media, schools, and the economy fell under state control. Czechoslovakia—which by this time was made up of the Czech Socialist Republic and the Slovak Socialist Republic—drew closer to the Soviet Union. The nation also joined the Warsaw Pact, a military alliance of Europe's Communist nations.

Following the Soviet model, Czechoslovakia's government took over manufacturing, banking, and agriculture. The regime set high production goals and also fixed prices as well as workers' wages. The nation imported energy fuels from the Soviet Union, which also provided a market for Czechoslovak goods. Under the new system, most laborers worked long hours for low pay.

In the countryside, farmers were forced to pool their land and machinery and to join cooperatives. Land seized by the regime became part of a system of state farms, on which farmers worked for wages. With little reward for increasing their harvests, farmers often failed to meet their production quotas.

In the early 1960s, Czechoslovakia's economy sharply declined. The government invested little in modernization, and factories grew obsolete. State farms and cooperatives did not increase their harvests, and food shortages occurred. As the country's living standards worsened, some Czech and Slovak officials called for a change in the nation's political and economic systems.

In response, President Antonín Novotný gave some businesses more freedom to set their own wages and prices. But Novotný refused to abandon central planning, to relax control of the media, or to legalize opposing political parties. In the mid-1960s, as the economy worsened, the president came under heavy criticism from within the Communist Party.

Alexander Dubcek, the leader of the Slovak Communist Party, challenged Novotný's reign. In January 1968, after winning support from other party members, Dubcek became the general secretary (leader) of the Czechoslovak Communist Party.

Under Dubcek's direction, the party lifted censorship and guaranteed freedom of religion and of the press throughout the country. Government controls over industries and farms eased, and the party promised increased independence for Slovakia. This period became known as the Prague Spring.

These actions greatly alarmed Soviet officials and other Warsaw Pact leaders, who saw the reform of Communism as a threat to their own regimes. On August 20, 1968, several Warsaw Pact nations invaded and occupied Czechoslovakia. Soviet officials then ordered the arrest of Dubcek, who was exiled. Gustav Husák—a close ally of the Soviet leadership—replaced Dubcek as the Czechoslovak general secretary.

Protesting the 1968 invasion of Czechoslovakia, a young Czech climbs onto a Soviet tank in Prague on August 21 of that year.

Husák Regime and the Velvet Revolution

In 1975 Husák became Czechoslovakia's president. Husák became one of the Soviet Union's closest allies in central Europe. At the same time, however, an organization emerged to fight for greater freedoms within Czechoslovakia. Called Charter 77, the group wrote a declaration protesting the harsh policies of the Husák regime. The leader of Charter 77 was Václav Havel, a playwright who criticized the government in many of his works.

Husák responded by imprisoning people who signed the document, including Havel. Those caught publishing or reading the works of Husák's opponents were also punished. Despite these actions, illegal underground writings became widely popular among Czech and Slovak students and workers.

> Charter 77 came into existence in January 1977, when more than two hundred Czech scholars published a petition announcing the formation of a group committed to human rights and the restoration of civil freedoms. Václav Havel was among these scholars. Western newspapers published the manifesto on January 6, and by the next day several of the charter's members had been arrested.

Although Czechoslovakia remained a strict Communist state, reforms were changing the Soviet Union. Mikhail Gorbachev, who became the Soviet leader in 1985, eased restrictions on the media and allowed some privately owned businesses to operate. People throughout the Warsaw Pact nations demanded similar changes in their countries. Husák, who refused to imitate Gorbachev's reforms, resigned as general secretary in 1987, but he remained Czechoslovakia's president.

In November 1989, several thousand opponents of the regime marched in Prague. A police attack on the demonstrators caused angry protests throughout the country. Husák named a new cabinet with a majority of non-Communist members. Civic Forum, an opposition movement, was formed to field non-Communist candidates for office.

The next month, a rally of 500,000 people and a general strike prompted Husák to resign. This period was called the Velvet Revolution because it brought about the bloodless overthrow of the country's Communist government. The legislature named Václav Havel as

Václav Havel

Graffiti scrawled in English on a kiosk in Prague shows Czechs' feelings about the fall of their Communist government in 1989.

Husák's successor, and in June 1990, free elections took place. Civic Forum and Public Against Violence—a Slovak opposition party—took power in the Czechoslovak legislature.

The problem of reforming the economy caused conflict in the new government. Some ministers favored the rapid transfer of state-run businesses to private owners, a process known as privatization. But Vladimír Mečiar, a Slovak politician, sought a slower transition for Slovakia. Mečiar claimed that privatization would greatly increase unemployment and poverty in Slovakia.

The new Czech leaders also argued for a strong central administration, with the government setting economic and foreign policy for Bohemia, Moravia, and Slovakia. But Mečiar and other Slovak politicians wanted more independence from the Prague government.

In 1992 Mečiar formed an independent Slovak government with himself as prime minister, and in January 1993 Slovakia became fully independent. The regions of Bohemia and Moravia made up the new Czech Republic. In 1993 Havel was elected as the first president of the Czech Republic.

Old and New Issues

Creating a new government was not the only task Czech leaders faced. They also needed to lay the groundwork for a new economy. Forced to rapidly privatize industries and to modernize the nation's banking system, many businesses and banks failed. Unemployment skyrocketed as struggling state-run factories and businesses were forced to shut down. The government did not have the resources to deal with other problems such as crime, corruption, and environmental pollution.

To make matters worse, in 1997 floodwaters covered most of Moravia. The flood destroyed homes and businesses, adding further pressure to an already strained economy. Inflation and unemployment rose, and the country's economy fell into a slump.

Ethnic tensions flared in August of that same year as hundreds of Roma (Gypsies) sought asylum in Canada, claiming they suffered persecution in the Czech Republic. The Roma are a nomadic people who may have originally come to Europe from India. Because of the Roma's nomadic lifestyle and their customs, many Czechs remain suspicious of them. To improve the situation, the Czech government created a commission for Roma affairs and outlined a plan for improving the Roma's situation.

After years of living under a strict Communist government, Czech leaders have come to the forefront of the world stage to address human rights. In 2000 the Czech Republic hosted Forum 2000, a conference that focused on protecting human rights around the world, promoting health and education for children, and preserving the environment.

Floodwaters again ravaged the Czech Republic in 2002 in one of the worst natural disasters the country has faced in the last 150 years. People lost their homes and businesses, and about fifty thousand people were forced to evacuate Prague. The disaster claimed more than one hundred lives across central and eastern Europe and caused an estimated $2 billion of damage to the country. The flood wiped out bridges, rail lines, utilities, and factories. This seriously affected the Czech Republic's already weakened economy. Parliament planned to raise taxes and cut costs wherever possible to help pay for the damage.

In August 2002, a rescue crew paddles through Prague's flooded streets in search of stranded or injured residents. For links to additional photos of the 2002 flooding, go to vgsbooks.com.

In addition, the government hoped to use international aid to build low-cost housing and to help small businesses in flooded areas.

The Czech Republic's cultural resources were also affected by the floodwaters, which damaged many famous historical buildings and museums in Prague and other cities. Czech officials estimated that it may take almost a century to restore the country's surviving historical treasures.

Government

The Czech parliament formally adopted a new constitution in December 1992. By its provisions, the Czech legislature consists of the Chamber of Deputies, whose two hundred members serve four-year terms, and the Senate, whose eighty-one members sit for six-year terms. Legislators have the power to enact laws, to approve a national budget, and to pass international treaties signed by the president. Adults older than eighteen years of age have the right to vote in legislative elections.

Both houses of the legislature elect the nation's president, who serves a five-year term. The president is the formal head of state and has the power to dissolve the legislature, to declare war, and to veto legislation. The president may not serve more than two consecutive terms.

The president appoints the prime minister, who is the administrative head of government. The prime minister sets the agenda for foreign and domestic policy and chooses government ministers.

The president, with the recommendations of the prime minister, appoints the seventeen members of the Council of Ministers. The council is the highest body of executive power, and its members direct the other government offices and ministries.

The judicial system consists of a supreme court, a constitutional court, an administrative court, and regional and district courts. The president names the fifteen judges of the Constitutional Court to ten-year terms. The Constitutional Court decides on legal matters of national importance.

The Czech Republic is divided into eight administrative regions. The city of Prague forms one of these regions. Each region, except for the capital, is further divided into several municipalities.

THE PEOPLE

Thousands of rural Czech families moved into cities after the end of World War II, and about 77 percent of the Czech Republic's 10.3 million people live in urban areas. The country's population density averages about 337 persons per square mile (131 per sq. km). Central Moravia and the industrialized regions of central and northern Bohemia have the highest densities. Mountainous areas have fewer cities and a much more scattered population.

The influx into the country's cities has led to urban overcrowding, causing housing shortages and higher rents. Family planning and contraceptives are widely used, and in 2001 the country's population growth declined to less than zero percent. At this rate, the projected population for 2050 will fall to 9.4 million.

Most city dwellers live in apartments, often with their extended families. Young people often live with their parents until their mid- to late twenties, when they typically establish their careers and get married. It is not uncommon for families to share living space with

their older relatives, and grandparents often baby-sit the younger children while both parents work.

People living in urban areas work in a variety of industries, especially factories and service jobs. Factory workers produce goods such as textiles, leather products, machinery, paper, and food products. As the country makes the shift to a free-market economy, more people are working in service jobs, employed by businesses like hotels, restaurants, and retail stores. Since the 1990s, new industries such as information technology and communications have taken on a large portion of the Czech workforce.

About 25 percent of the rural families who do work on farms own their land. Other farmers work for state-owned farms or for cooperatives. On family farms, fathers typically act as the head of the household and make most of the decisions. Men generally work in the fields, while women and girls tend the household. Both men and women care for the livestock.

Many urban Czechs live in **high-rise apartment complexes** such as these in Prague. Most of the buildings were constructed during the Communist era.

Living in Czech cities usually means living in high-rise apartments. Whether they live in a house or an apartment, however, Czechs take pride in their homes. They usually remove their shoes at the door and don slippers. Homes often have indoor plants or small garden boxes.

Housing in urban areas is expensive and in short supply, so several generations of a family often live together. To save space in smaller homes, many people have special beds that can be turned into sofas during the day, similar to a futon. Some of the wealthier city-dwellers keep a second home in the country.

In rural areas, some Czechs work as farmers, but most rural workers have jobs in the mining or forestry industry or at power plants. Rural families, which are usually larger than city families, often live in farmhouses, where they have larger living areas than city-dwellers.

Ethnic Groups

Ethnic Czechs—Bohemians and Moravians—are descended from ancient Slavic groups who invaded central Europe in the fifth century A.D. The Slavic Czechs migrated into the valleys and lowlands of Bohemia and Moravia, where many other ethnic groups—including Poles, Hungarians, Germans, and Slovaks—later settled. But the treaties that ended the world wars of the twentieth century forced many non-Czechs to move out of the country. Most Sudeten Germans, for example, were exiled to Germany after the end of World War II.

The Czechs form 90 percent of the Czech Republic's population,

A Roma family makes its way through the streets of Prague.

THE ROMA

The Roma make up a small part of the Czech population. They are often called Gypsies, a name that comes from the Middle Ages (A.D. 500–1500), when people believed they came from Egypt. The Roma are probably descendants of Indian immigrants, however. Their language is known as Romany.

Most Roma have olive skin and are slightly built. They often travel in small clans led by elders. They make their living as metalworkers, singers, dancers, and auto mechanics. Roma women are famous as fortune-tellers. The Roma usually adopt the religion of their country of residence.

The Roma have retained their own language, dress, nomadic life, and customs. Because of this and their refusal to conform to many of the customs of the majority, the Roma have faced discrimination across Europe for centuries. In many European countries, laws have been passed outlawing Roma customs and language, and attempts have been made to force them to give up their nomadic lifestyle.

and Moravians account for 3 percent. Ethnic Slovaks make up 2 percent of the nation's population. About 1 percent of the total population claim German or Polish ancestry. The Czech Republic also has a small population of Roma, a nomadic people who may have originally come to Europe from India.

The Czech Republic is home to a small community of Vietnamese, who came to the land during the Communist era and who refused to return to Vietnam after the Velvet Revolution. Jews are also a small minority group. About six thousand Jews live in the Czech Republic, many in Prague.

◉ Language

Like the Czech people, the Czech language has a long, and sometimes turbulent, history. The Czech language belongs to the Western Slavic family, a group that also

Cyril and Methodius created the Cyrillic alphabet, which is still used for Russian and other eastern European languages. Their work is remembered through this statue on Prague's Charles Bridge, which shows them with some young followers.

includes Slovak and Polish. While the Slavic tribes that settled in Bohemia and Moravia had a common spoken language for centuries, a written form of the language did not exist until the Christian missionaries Cyril and Methodius developed a Slavic alphabet in the late 800s. These Byzantine monks, who arrived in the area in 863, taught the Slavs Christian prayers and rituals in the Slavic language. To translate the Bible into this tongue, Cyril and Methodius also devised a new lettering system known as the Cyrillic alphabet.

German replaced the Czech language after the Czechs were defeated in the Thirty Years' War (1618–1648). While their literature was stifled, however, most rural Czechs continued to use the spoken language. During the nationalist movement of the late 1700s, Czech scholars began once again to use the written form of the Czech language. In the nineteenth and twentieth centuries, Czechs recognized the importance of language to their cultural heritage. When the independent country of Czechoslovakia emerged in 1918, the people chose Czech as their official language. It has remained the common language of the Czech people.

Czech speakers—especially those living in rural areas—have developed several local dialects. The Moravian dialect, for example, includes both Czech and Slovak expressions. Most members of ethnic minorities—including Germans and Poles—speak a second language in addition to Czech. Many Czech schoolchildren also learn English in secondary school.

The Czech language actually has two forms. S*pisovna cestina*—the formal, written Czech—is used in the media and for instruction at

Czech universities. For everyday conversation, most people use *hovorova*, an informal Czech that is full of slang words and expressions. Unlike the written language, spoken Czech includes some German and English words.

The Czech language has loaned words to other languages, including English. *Polka, pistol,* and *robot* are a few of the Czech words that have become common in English.

⊙ Health

After World War II, the health care system in Czechoslovakia was placed under state control. Doctors and nurses became state employees, and the government made free health care and medicine available to citizens. But as the economy stalled, the state stopped buying new medical equipment for clinics and hospitals, and health care standards declined.

In the early 1990s, the new government began privatizing hospitals and clinics and legalized private medical insurance companies. A tightly managed budget has provided health care workers with the latest medical technology and drugs.

Independent insurance companies pay for health care services, and these companies fall under tight state supervision. The Ministry of Health supervises health care legislation, medical research and technology, and runs nursing schools. It also manages regional hospitals and other health care facilities and monitors the nation's natural spas and sources of mineral waters.

MINERAL WATERS

The Bohemian countryside has many mineral springs, naturally occurring streams with large deposits of dissolved minerals. Believed to have healing powers, these springs have been developed into spa towns. Guests at these spas treat a variety of medical conditions by bathing in the hot springs or drinking water from the springs.

The oldest and most famous of these spa towns is Karlovy Vary in Bohemia. According to legend, Charles IV discovered the springs in the fourteenth century during a hunting excursion. He immediately commissioned the building of a castle and named the place Karlovy Vary, or Charles's Boiling Place.

The town of Karlovy Vary has attracted tourists to its spas for centuries.

The insurance system generally insures family members separately and is financed by workers and their employers. Participation in the system is compulsory, meaning everyone must contribute. The state contributes to insurance for unemployed people, students, and children.

Average life expectancy in the Czech Republic has reached 75 years, second only to Slovenia for former Soviet bloc countries. The infant mortality rate—the number of babies who die within one year of their birth—is 4.1 per every 1,000 live births, one of the lowest rates in the world. But the country's birthrate has fallen, and the rate of population growth is less than zero. Young people are waiting longer to get married and have children, and family size is also smaller than in the 1950s and 1960s. In the future, this trend will force Czech workers to support an expanding population of aging retirees.

The country's health care system faces new challenges. With funding going mostly to new equipment and prescription drugs, hospitals and clinics lack the money to reconstruct outdated facilities. And the country's highly trained doctors and nurses receive some of the lowest salaries among the country's professional workforce. As a result, many move to other countries for employment.

Education

Education has long been an important part of Czech life. The oldest university in central Europe is Charles University in Prague, which dates to 1348. The nation has enjoyed nearly 100 percent literacy since the early 1900s. The Czechs consider education important, and children are encouraged to do well in school.

Women have played a major role in Czech history, enjoying a certain degree of political power. They typically have equal opportunities in areas such as education. However, while Czech women make up about half the workforce, they earn only about 70 percent of what men earn.

In the past, Czech education was influenced by the country's rulers and political systems. The Hapsburgs forced Czech students, teachers, and textbook authors to use the German language. Under Communism, teachers trained their students in socialist philosophy, which glorified farmers and laborers and criticized the wealthy. Religious and private schools were outlawed, while the government encouraged students from working-class families to attend public universities. Many upper-class students were denied postsecondary education.

At Charles University in Prague, students and professors in formal academic dress participate in a graduation ceremony.

After the Communist government relinquished power, the new Czech government legalized private and religious schools and reduced government influence in the classroom. However, the government still fully funds primary and secondary schools.

From the age of three, Czech children typically attend three years of *materska skola* , or preschool. From the ages of six to fifteen, Czech children must attend *zakladni skola*, or primary school. After this, they may enter a vocational school or a four-year school that prepares them for university studies. The nation has twenty-three institutions for higher education, including four universities.

If you'd like to find out more about the people of the Czech Republic, go to vgsbooks.com, where you'll find links to websites that have information on various ethnic groups and the Czech language and lifestyle.

CULTURAL LIFE

The Czech Republic lies at the political and cultural crossroads of Europe. Before the Communist era, Prague was an important cultural center. The republic's rich ethnic mixture and long history have shaped its arts, giving them a unique flavor. Czech contributions to literature, music, and theater have enjoyed international success.

◎ Religion

Christianity was probably first introduced to Bohemia and Moravia in the late 700s, yet it wasn't until the 1100s that the Czech population became largely Roman Catholic. Nearly 40 percent of the republic's citizens are Catholics, although there has been a large minority of Czech Protestants since the Protestant Reformation of the 1500s. The Reformed Church and the Czech Brethren are two important Protestant churches. Other Christian churches include the Old Catholic Church, the Hussite Church, and the Eastern Orthodox Church. Prague once included a large Jewish population, but most Czech Jews

were sent to Nazi concentration camps during World War II.

The Communist government saw religion as a dangerous rival for the loyalty of Czech citizens. Antireligious teachings became part of state-sponsored schools. Many Czechs stopped attending services, and many of the nation's churches fell into disrepair or were closed.

After the fall of the Communist government in 1989, Czech churches again opened their doors to worshipers. Churches have gained new followers, and Christian missionaries from other countries have arrived to win converts. In addition, crews are busy restoring historic churches and cathedrals. Despite this religious revival, almost 40 percent of young people remain atheists (people who deny the existence of God).

Holidays and Festivals

Czech festivals are a combination of religious, cultural, and nationalistic traditions. While many festivals are celebrated nationwide, some are observed only in certain regions or villages.

At the **International Folklore Festival** in Strážnice, Czech dancers in traditional garb perform to the tune of a folk melody.

Almost every day of the year is a name day, a day named after a Catholic saint. For example, September 28 is Saint Wenceslas's Day. People often give gifts or cards to friends and family members who share the saint's name on these days.

The two most important Christian religious holidays are Christmas and Easter, which commemorate the birth, death, and resurrection of Jesus Christ, who Christians believe is the Son of God. The Christmas season begins on December 6, Saint Nicholas's Day. Children receive a visit from friends or family members dressed up as Saint Nicholas and the devil. Saint Nicholas wears a white hat and a long coat. The devil wears a mask or black makeup, horns, and a fur coat.

December 25 and December 26, also called First Christmas and Second Christmas, are state holidays. Families come together to exchange gifts and share meals, traditionally carp and roasted turkey.

The Easter celebration takes place in March or April, starting with Palm Sunday. Priests bless pussy willows, symbols of new life, and people place the willow branches in their windows. Some Czechs decorate eggs with bright colors and elaborate designs.

A popular modern celebration is the International Folklore Festival in Strážnice, Moravia. This two-day affair, founded in 1945, has helped preserve traditional Czech dress, music, and dance. Festivities include musical performances, ethnic food, and beer and wine.

National holidays include Independence Day on October 28, the anniversary of the founding of the first Czechoslovak Republic in 1918; Liberation Day on May 8, which commemorates the liberation of Prague from the Nazis in 1945; and January 1, the anniversary of the creation of the Czech Republic in 1993.

Food

Czechs enjoy a hearty cuisine known for its roasted meats, wild game, pickled vegetables, dumplings, and pastries. Czech cooks have incorporated many dishes from neighboring countries over the years. Goulash, a meat stew spiced with paprika, arrived from Hungary. Sauerkraut (pickled cabbage) and goose came from Germany, and Austria contributed schnitzel, a breaded veal cutlet. Sour cream, vinegar, and pickled vegetables from Slavic countries to the east add flavor and variety to Czech meals.

One of the most popular Czech meals includes pork, sauerkraut, and the widely popular *knedliky* (dumplings) that accompany many main dishes and soups. To make knedliky, Czech cooks boil or steam a mixture of flour, eggs, milk, and dried bread crumbs. Dumplings may have fillings of plums or other fruit.

Appetizers include smoked meats, herring, sardines, or pickles. Czech chefts often prepare roasted goose or duck and game meats such as hare and venison (deer meat). Carp is traditionally served at Christmas.

VANILKOVE ROHLICKY (VANILLA CRESCENTS)

These popular cookies are eaten at Christmas in the Czech Republic.

½ lb. (2 sticks) unsalted butter, softened	1¼ c. ground, unblanched almonds
½ c. sugar	1 tsp. vanilla extract
2 c. flour	½ tsp. salt
	confectioners' sugar

1. Cream butter and sugar. Add flour, ½ cup at a time.
2. Stir in almonds, vanilla extract, and salt. Mix until dough becomes slightly stiff.
3. Form the dough into a ball. Wrap in wax paper and refrigerate for one hour.
4. Once chilled, pinch off pieces of dough about 1 inch thick. On a floured board, roll each piece into a strip 1 inch wide and ½ inch thick.
5. Shape each strip into a crescent by pulling it into a semicircle. Place on a lightly buttered baking sheet.
6. Bake for 15 to 20 minutes in a 350° oven. Once removed from the oven, leave crescents to cool on the baking sheet for 5 minutes. Transfer to a cooling rack.
7. Dust with confectioners' sugar.

For dessert, Czechs enjoy pastries, fruit-filled pancakes, and cream or chocolate cakes. With their meals, adults sometimes drink beer—the best comes from the town of Plzeň—or red wines from Moravia. *Slivovice,* or plum brandy, is a favorite after-dinner beverage.

Music

Prague has been an important center for the country's music scene since at least the seventeenth century. By the late eighteenth century, the city boasted several opera houses and was the opening stage for some of Mozart's famous operas. The Czech Philharmonic Orchestra, founded in 1896, is still considered one of the world's top symphony orchestras.

Many Czech musicians have gained world recognition for their works while drawing on their cultural heritage. Bedřich Smetana (1824–1884) wrote symphonies and operas using Bohemian folktales and legends. Smetana's work *Má Vlast (My Country)* helped inspire Czech nationalism in the late nineteenth century. Internationally renowned composer Antonín Dvořák, the composer of *Moravian Duets* and *Slavonic Dances,* wrote his famous symphony, entitled *From the New World,* in the United States. Dvořák also composed operas, choral music, string trios and quartets, and piano works that received worldwide acclaim.

In addition to classical and folk music, modern music has also become quite popular. Jazz and rock bands became a leading voice of political opposition during the 1980s, when several underground rock and jazz clubs opened in Prague. Czech cities still have large audiences for rock, jazz, and classical music. The Prague Spring Music Festival is

Bedřich Smetana wrote music about the Vltava River and other Czech themes. His statue stands near the river in Prague.

Composer **Antonín Dvořák** drew inspiration for his work from Czech folk music.

one of Europe's biggest annual musical events. During this extravaganza, audiences crowd the capital's restored theaters and concert halls to enjoy opera, ballet, and symphonic music.

Modern Czech musicians, like keyboardist Jan Hamr, are still reaching an international audience. Hamr immigrated to the United States in the 1970s and became jazz-rock composer Jan Hammer. He composes for television shows, commercials, and movies. His most famous work is the theme song for the television show *Miami Vice.*

Literature

Czech literature dates to the early thirteenth century, when writers began recording legends, histories, and stories in the Czech language. In the 1400s, when the first Czech books were printed, the religious reformer Jan Hus published works of theology and important studies of Czech grammar and language.

When the German-speaking Hapsburgs took over Bohemia and Moravia, their ban on Czech writing nearly destroyed the nation's literature. A reawakening of nationalism in the late 1700s and early 1800s started with František Palacký's *History of Bohemia.* Other scholars, like Josef Dobrovsky and Josef Jungmann, further sparked a revival of Czech writing by introducing the study of Czech in schools, where the Hapsburgs had imposed German. During the 1830s, Jungmann compiled a new Czech dictionary that inspired poets and novelists to use the Czech language in their works.

Czech writers of this time penned narrative poems, folktales, and histories. Karel Mácha, considered the finest Czech poet of his day, wrote *Maj (May),* a long poem about love and death. Other writers described the everyday lives and experiences of the Czech people. For example, Božena Nemcová drew on Czech peasant life in her

Franz Kafka

innovative novels and tales. These literary themes changed in the early 1900s with the works of Franz Kafka, a Jewish author who lived in Prague. The characters in Kafka's novels and stories, which include *The Trial*, *Metamorphosis*, and *The Castle*, suffer fear and bewilderment in the face of modern civilization. Rainer Maria Rilke, another writer from Prague, used complex symbols and imagery in his poetry.

Czechoslovakia's Communist regime tried to silence writers who expressed any criticism of the government or its policies. Many writers left the country, while others were imprisoned. Milan Kundera, Josef Skvorecky, and Ivan Klima are skilled Czech writers who won an international audience for their novels and stories. But only Klima stayed in Czechoslovakia for the duration of the Communist era.

Contemporary Czech writers continue to make contributions to world literature. Czech poet Jaroslav Seifert received the Nobel Prize in 1984. Women writers such as Eda Kriseova and Alexandra Berkova are also important to modern Czech literature.

Theater

Theater has played an important role in Czech cultural life, from the earliest religious dramas to the political plays of modern playwrights. Money for the 1883 opening of the National Theater in Prague came from donations from rich and poor Czechs alike. In the seventeenth century, the scholar Jan Ămos Komenský used drama to teach philosophy and other contemporary issues to his students.

Before the twentieth century, many Czech playwrights used patriotic themes and folk stories in their works. Under Communism, sarcastic comic plays gained a wide audience in underground theaters. Václav Havel, a famous playwright working in underground theater, spent several years in prison for mocking the regime. Since the fall of the Communist government, new theater groups have emerged and the modern Czech Republic has dozens of theaters that stage both modern and classical plays.

Puppetry remains a popular theater form for young and old audiences. Puppet theater in Bohemia dates back to the seventeenth century. The art underwent a revival in the 1920s, when Josef Skupa created his legendary puppets, Špejbel and Hurvínek.

Architecture

Like other Czech art forms, Czech architecture is a combination of many styles. Modern cities such as Prague, virtually untouched by two world wars, feature a unique combination of ancient and modern buildings. Plain but solid Romanesque churches, built in the ninth century, stand proudly amid modern office buildings and high-rise apartments.

Thirteenth and fourteenth century Gothic structures—with their high ceilings, elaborate doorway columns, and stained glass windows—still draw crowds of visitors. The most famous of these include Prague's Saint Vitus Cathedral and the Old Town Bridge Tower of Charles Bridge.

After the Thirty Years' War, Czech architects were commissioned to restore damaged buildings. Huge wall paintings and elaborate gold ornamentation were often added after these restorations.

In the twentieth century, Czech architects returned to a simpler style. Elegant modern buildings with clean lines became popular during the first half of the century. The country's rich architectural heritage changed, however, when the Communist regime seized power. From the 1950s to the 1980s, buildings were created for function. Massive housing projects and concrete government buildings stood side-by-side with the decorative architecture of past centuries. Government officials ordered many of the older buildings to be plastered over to match the new buildings.

After the fall of Communism, the new Czech government

It took nearly six hundred years to complete work on **Saint Vitus Cathedral** in Prague. Construction began in 1344 and was finished in 1929.

commissioned the removal of the Communist plasterwork to restore the original architecture. Because many of these buildings were in need of repair, the government also set aside money for the restoration and conservation of the country's architectural legacy. The floods of 2002 seriously damaged the country's architecture, however, further challenging restoration attempts.

◎ The Arts

Czech artists typically followed the trends of Western Europe. While Czech artists were considered some of the best in Europe, Czech art contributed few unique ideas or techniques until the Czech national revival of the late eighteenth and early nineteenth centuries. This movement became known as Czech Realism. Artists working in this style focused on ethnic dress and traditions, creating detailed images of everyday objects and scenes. They also turned to Czech folklore for subject matter, depicting scenes from the country's myths and legends. Many artists of this time became international names, such as illustrator Alfons Mucha and painter Josef Capek.

While the Nazis, and later the Communists, suppressed freedom of expression, modern Czech artists are once again enjoying international fame. Artists such as Milena Dopitiva and Karel Pokorny are bringing Prague to the forefront of the world art scene with their dramatic works.

Czech folk arts have also experienced a revival. Folk arts are based on the country's local customs, including traditional crafts, clothing, and music. These traditions are passed down through families from one generation to the next and through folk festivals. Folk arts vary from region to region, each with its own unique designs. Folk costumes, for example, often include elaborate embroidery in bright colors and geometric patterns. The designs and color combinations are unique to each region. Wood carvings and

BOX ART

Under the Communists, artists and their works were censored by the government. In 1984 artist Joska Skalnik devised a plan that eventually allowed artists to freely exhibit their creations without government interference. Skalnik invited artists to create works that would fit inside small wooden boxes. Once he received these mini-galleries, Skalnik hid them in a shed outside of Prague. They were kept there until the Velvet Revolution in 1989. Since 1992, the works have been exhibited all over the world. In 1993 the Czech government declared the box art a national treasure.

small sculptures are also popular forms of folk art.

Another way Czechs preserve their folk traditions is through open-air museums known as *skansens*. These museums feature traditional home architecture and furnishings. The larger skansens exhibit how entire communities lived through the buildings, wares, and clothing typical of a period.

Recreation and Sports

The forests, mountains, and lakes of Bohemia offer Czechs many opportunities for outdoor recreation. The country has downhill and cross-country skiing areas, and the mountains also draw rock climbers. Hikers can follow networks of marked trails in the Jeseník Mountains and in other highland regions.

Waterskiing and windsurfing are popular in the lakes of southern Bohemia, including lakes formed by dams along the Vltava River. The rapids of the Vltava and Labe Rivers, as well as smaller streams in the mountains, challenge canoeists and kayakers.

Tennis has long been the favorite sport of young Czechs. Nearly every Czech town has tennis courts and organized clubs. The country has produced many international tennis champions, including Ivan Lendl, Hana Mandlikova, Martina Navratilová, and Jana Novotna. The Czechs are also enthusiastic soccer players. Thousands of adults and young people join local soccer teams. Other team sports—including ice hockey, volleyball, and basketball—draw large crowds. At the 1998 winter Olypmics, Czechs cheered as the men's ice hockey team beat the rival Russian team to win a gold medal.

Many tennis enthusiasts view **Martina Navratilová** *(pictured at right before her retirement in 1994)* as one of the greatest tennis players of all time. Born in Prague, she later became a U.S. citizen.

THE ECONOMY

The Czech Republic ranks as one of the most industrialized countries in Europe. The nation's large manufacturing sector dates from the eighteenth century, when Bohemia and Moravia made up the industrial heartland of the Hapsburg Empire. The rich soils of Bohemia and Moravia also allow intensive farming, and the Czechs have mined coal and other minerals for centuries.

The Czech economy underwent a drastic change after World War II, when the new Communist government seized the nation's factories, farms, and mines. The government closely controlled the economy by setting prices, wages, and production levels. Through a series of five-year plans, Communist officials attempted to manage the supply of goods to meet demand. New factories were built in Plzeň, Brno, and other cities, and the manufacturing sector employed a growing percentage of Czech workers.

But with their wages fixed, workers had little incentive to increase their production. With an emphasis on quantity rather than quality,

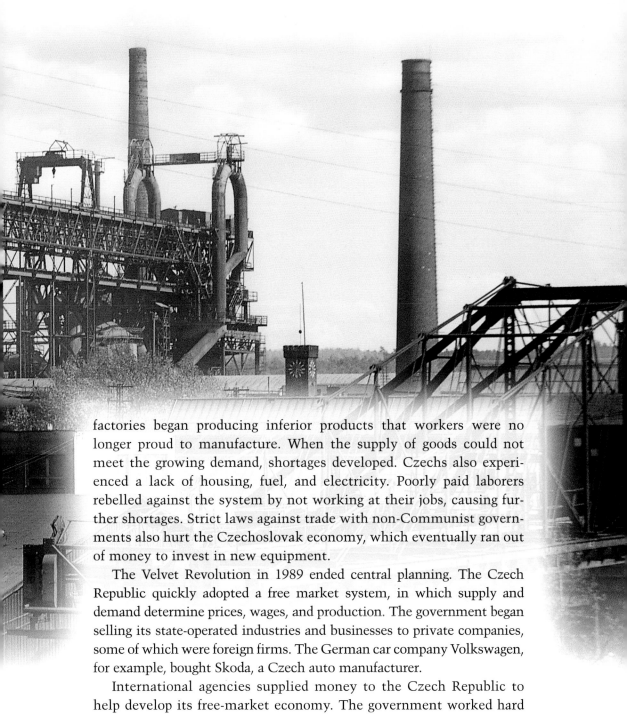

factories began producing inferior products that workers were no longer proud to manufacture. When the supply of goods could not meet the growing demand, shortages developed. Czechs also experienced a lack of housing, fuel, and electricity. Poorly paid laborers rebelled against the system by not working at their jobs, causing further shortages. Strict laws against trade with non-Communist governments also hurt the Czechoslovak economy, which eventually ran out of money to invest in new equipment.

The Velvet Revolution in 1989 ended central planning. The Czech Republic quickly adopted a free market system, in which supply and demand determine prices, wages, and production. The government began selling its state-operated industries and businesses to private companies, some of which were foreign firms. The German car company Volkswagen, for example, bought Skoda, a Czech auto manufacturer.

International agencies supplied money to the Czech Republic to help develop its free-market economy. The government worked hard to offer incentives for foreign companies, such as waiving taxes for ten years, allowing equipment into the country duty-free, and paying workers as they receive job training.

The transition to a market economy has not always been smooth, however. Obsolete companies that could not compete in the new economy closed, and many laborers lost their jobs. In addition, the lifting of price controls caused a sharp rise in the cost of living. In 1997 the economy fell into a recession and the government was forced to devalue the currency.

The Czech Republic joined the United Nations in 1993 and has applied for membership in the European Union (EU), an economic alliance of European nations. In 1995 the country joined the Organization for Economic Cooperation and Development, an international organization that promotes economic cooperation among its member countries.

> The Czech workday usually begins at 8 A.M. and ends between 3 and 4:30 P.M., Monday through Friday. Shops stay open later, until 5 or 6 P.M. An influx of foreign companies has extended the workday for some, which many Czechs do not like. Czech jobs range from factory work to health care and other services. A growing number of people work in computers and information systems. Farming and mining still employ a small percent of the Czech workforce.

During the 1990s, thousands of young Americans, drawn by the city's expanding financial opportunities, came to Prague to open businesses. Many of the new, privately owned businesses used computers, creating a need for computers and software that helped develop the Czech Republic's high-tech sector.

Despite some setbacks, the new economy resulted in higher wages and better living standards for many workers. Gross domestic product (GDP)—the amount of goods and services produced by the country in a year—slowly increased. By 1998 the country's GDP was $54.5 billion. Trade with western Europe rose, and tax breaks and other incentives attracted thousands of foreign investors to the country. By the new millennium, more than 85 percent of the country's businesses were privately owned. Government subsidies to ailing businesses and rent-controlled housing helped ease the shock of the transition for those workers employed by outdated state industries.

By 1999, following an increase in exports and foreign investment, the economy began to recover. Foreign investment from countries such as Germany, the Netherlands, and the United States brought $5 billion into the Czech Republic that same year.

In addition to bringing in foreign revenue, the government has worked to establish strong political and commercial ties. In 1999 the Czech Republic became a North Atlantic Treaty Organization (NATO) member. The Czechs continue to form trade partnerships with their neighbors in central Europe, including Hungary and Poland. These actions should bring increased investment and production and eventually provide a better standard of living for the Czech people. In 2002 the government voted to increase the minimum wage to motivate workers and to help reduce the number of people on social benefits.

In August 2002, heavy floods hit the country, affecting agricultural, industrial, and tourist areas. Damage was estimated around $2 billion, which will likely take a toll on social spending. The purchase of new jet fighters was immediately cut to help cover the cost of damages.

The flood will also adversely affect the economy by reducing economic growth. It will take years to recover certain important sectors, particularly tourism and manufacturing. This, in turn, will increase the country's budget deficit and increase inflation. While economic growth is expected to recover in 2003 with the help of foreign investment and aid, time will determine the floodwaters' full impact on the country's economy.

◉ Manufacturing

The busy Czech industrial sector dates to the years of Hapsburg rule, when Bohemia provided the empire with munitions and weaponry. After the Communist government nationalized (brought under government control) most industries, the country suffered a sharp decline

These women assemble cars at the Skoda factory.

GLASSWARE

Czech glassmakers, especially in Bohemia, are world renowned for their engraved glassware and crystal. The art began in the thirteenth century in northwestern Bohemia. Glassmakers heated sand and quartz over fires, then blew it into shapes using hollow rods or by pouring it into clay molds. During the 1600s, Bohemian crafters developed new techniques and added limestone to their glass, which made their creations sparkle more. From there, artisans cut, colored, or engraved their product. In cut-glass vases, designs may include thousands of cuts. Bohemian artisans soon became world famous for their work, and Czech glassware was imported throughout Europe, the Middle East, and the Americas. While most glassware produced in the Czech Republic is created in factories, Czech glassware is still considered some of the best in the world.

in manufacturing. In the 1960s, factory managers had no authority to make decisions that could have improved the efficiency or productivity of their plants. In addition, because the nation did not trade or compete with western Europe, there was little need for modernization. By the mid-1980s, most of the country's industrial machinery was obsolete.

In the early 1990s, the new government sold thousands of state-owned enterprises to private firms. At first only Czech citizens could buy shares in the newly privatized companies. Later the government invited foreign companies to bid for ownership. In April 1993, the Czech Republic reopened its stock exchange, through which the public can buy and sell company shares.

Czech industry steadily declined in the 1990s. By 1998 only about 40 percent of the country's GDP came from manufacturing, which employs 40 percent of the workforce. Important products include processed foods, machinery, iron and steel, transportation equipment, chemicals, and petroleum.

The Czech Republic also has a healthy and growing light industry sector that produces beer, ceramics, clothing, paper, and textiles. Plzeň is a major brewing center, and workshops in northern Bohemia have been making glass since the 1200s. Czech factories also turn out shoes, iron and steel, and textiles.

Agriculture

The Czech Republic is rich with fertile land, and nearly half of the country is suitable for farming. But agriculture contributed only 4 percent of the GDP in 1998.

At a market in Brno, **a woman sells produce** grown by Czech farmers.

After World War II, the Communist government created collective farms, where farmers shared their labor, equipment, and land. The government also set up large state farms—public acreages that paid fixed salaries to farmers regardless of how much or how little they produced. The low pay on collective and state farms prompted thousands of people to abandon farming and move to the cities, where they joined the better-paying manufacturing sector. This migration hurt agricultural production, and food gradually became scarce throughout the country.

State and collective farms still exist in the new Czech Republic, but 80 percent of the country's farmland is privately owned. The free-market economy, in which farmers can set prices for their goods, has helped end shortages and has improved the earnings of most Czech farmers. By 1999, however, less than 6 percent of the workforce was involved in farming.

The Czech Republic's most important crops are sugar beets, potatoes, wheat, and barley. Bohemia is one of the world's largest producers of hops, a main ingredient in beer. Livestock—hogs, cattle, and poultry—are also important agricultural products.

Energy and Mining

For many years, Czechoslovakia bought inexpensive electricity and fuel from the Soviet Union. As a member of the Soviet bloc, the nation was also able to import crude oil at low, controlled prices. Cheap fuel made Czechoslovakia dependent on Soviet energy imports yet shielded the country from rises in the market price of oil.

When the Soviet bloc collapsed, the Czech Republic suddenly had to pay much higher energy prices on an open market. At the same time, the growing economy increased the need for fuel and electricity

The **Temelin nuclear plant** began supplying power for parts of the Czech Republic in 2000.

to power factories. To meet demand, the Czech government adopted a conservation program and began construction of two nuclear power stations.

In the mid-1990s, the Czech Republic was producing much more of its own energy at coal-burning and nuclear plants. By 1998, 75 percent of the country's energy came from power stations using coal, 20 percent came from nuclear plants, and the rest came from hydroelectric generation. To further conserve its supply of coal, the country opened two reactors at the Temelin nuclear plant in 2000.

Mining employs about 2 percent of the workforce and plays a small but important role in the Czech economy. Coal deposits in Bohemia and northern Moravia offer a plentiful source of fuel for power plants. One of Europe's largest reserves of uranium ore lies in the Ore Mountains of northwestern Bohemia, where miners also extract antimony, tin, and mercury.

Foreign Trade

Under Communism, the nation traded exclusively with its Warsaw Pact allies. Without competition from western Europe, some Czech factories and products grew obsolete. Under the new economic system, the government is trying to produce a wider range of products and to attract foreign investors to retool outdated plants for other uses.

To increase its exports, the Czech government is building new trade alliances. The Czech Republic and Slovakia have formed a customs union, meaning the two nations do not tax goods exchanged between them. Poland, Hungary, the Czech Republic, and Slovakia have also set up a trading partnership.

Almost 70 percent of all Czech exports go to members of the European Union (EU), a trade organization that the Czech Republic wishes to join. This would greatly increase the market for Czech goods and could spur further foreign investment in the country.

Transportation and Tourism

The Czech Republic has a well developed transportation system, due largely to the efforts of the former Communist government. After World War II, the government commissioned the building of new railways, highways, and airports. By 1998 Czech State Railways had a rail route that ran 5,804 miles (9,341 km). Passenger trains and light-rail networks run through Prague, Brno, Liberec, Most, Olomouc, Plzeň, and Ostrava.

The Czechs have an extensive system of highways and public transportation. In 1998 more than 12,427 miles (20,000 km) of highways and main roads crisscrossed the country. The government is planning to build new and better roadways, although less than half of the population own cars. The nation is also improving its road links to other European countries. The national airline, Czech Airlines, provides direct flights to European and North American cities from Ruzyne airport near Prague.

Czechoslovakia was one of the first Communist European countries to open its borders to tourists. Tourism thrived after the fall of Communism. Since the early 1990s, thousands of Czech citizens have set up shops, hotels, and other businesses that cater to foreign travelers. In 2001, 103 million tourists from other countries visited the Czech Republic. This has helped the services sector—including retail shops, hotels, and travel agents.

GETTING AROUND

Although the Czech Republic has a well developed road system, less than half of the population own cars. Because of the high cost of buying and owning a car, many people stick to public transportation, especially buses. Bus networks connect suburbs to cities, and some cover even longer distances. Trains also offer commuters a lift, but they are typically not as clean or reliable as buses. Larger cities such as Prague also have subways and trolleys (below).

A crowd of tourists gazes at the **astronomical clock that adorns Prague's Old Town Hall.** According to legend, the clock maker's eyes were gouged out after the clock's completion so that he could never make another clock of equal beauty.

Prague, where many historic streets and buildings have survived, remains the most popular destination in the country. Crowds of tourists visit Prague Castle, the Charles Bridge, and the famous clock tower in the Old Town neighborhood.

Outside of the capital, ancient castles dot the Bohemian countryside, and the artificial lakes along the Vltava River attract boaters and campers. Moravia is well known for its vineyards and wine cellars. East of Brno are the famous fields of Slavkov, where Napoleon defeated the Hapsburg army in the Battle of Austerlitz.

The Future

The Czech Republic's peaceful transition from Communism to democracy has made it one of the most successful of the former Soviet-bloc countries. Privately owned businesses have replaced almost 90 percent of the state-run collectives of the Communist years. Adopting a democratic government and a free-market system has improved foreign trade and production, and the growing economy is improving the nation's standard of living.

Yet the young nation must overcome important obstacles. The country's banking and communications systems desperately need to be modernized, and the political system has not yet found solutions or resources to deal with many of the country's immediate problems.

Economic woes continue to impact the country. The Czech Republic's economy suffered a severe recession in 1997 due to rising inflation and unemployment. Unemployed workers must find and train for new jobs as the government continues to privatize and modernize state industries. The free market has also forced the country's citizens to pay higher prices for energy and food, and housing shortages plague the nation's cities. In addition, the 2002 floods will affect the nation's economy for years to come.

The economic situation has led to social problems such as ethnic tension and higher crime rates. In addition, inefficient energy use has damaged the nation's air, water, and soil. Many Czech cities suffer pollution problems that threaten potential foreign investments. These problems must be solved before the Czech Republic can fully realize its potential as an independent democratic nation.

While the Czech Republic has made huge strides since it emerged in 1993, the transition to a new economic and political system will continue to take time and effort. But the Czechs eagerly embrace these changes, proud to be in control of their present and their future.

Visit vgsbooks.com for up-to-date information about the economy of the Czech Republic. You'll also find a converter with the current exchange rate that tells you how many Czech koruna are in a U.S. dollar.

4000 B.C.	A group of people settle in the area that later becomes Prague.
200s B.C.	The Boii, nomadic Celts, arrive in Bohemia.
A.D. 400s	Czechs, a Slavic group of people, migrate to Bohemia.
623	Samo establishes the first independent Slavic state in Bohemia.
833	Mojmir unites parts of Bohemia, Moravia, Poland, and Slovakia to create the Great Moravian Empire.
863	Christian missionaries Cyril and Methodius come to the area. They develop the Cyrillic alphabet.
CA. 900	Přemyslid dynasty is founded.
1278	Rudolf II brings Bohemia under Hapsburg control.
1330s	Construction begins on Prague Castle.
1348	Charles IV establishes the University of Prague.
1411	Jan Hus rebels against the Catholic Church, creating the Hussite movement.
1547	Emperor Ferdinand claims Bohemia as a Hapsburg territory.
1618	Czech nobles spark the Thirty Years' War.
1648	The Treaty of Westphalia ends the Thirty Years' War.
1780	Joseph II takes the throne and makes reforms to the Hapsburg Empire.
1800	The Prague Academy for Fine Arts is founded.
1818	The National Museum is founded in Prague.
1834	Josef K. Tyl composes his famous "Song Number 19," which later becomes the Czech national anthem.
1836	Karel Mácha writes his epic poem *Maj (May)*.
1878	Antonín Dvořák publishes the first set of his *Slavonic Dances*.
1883	The National Theater opens in Prague.
1918	An independent Czechoslovak nation is created.
1925	The Czech people's first open-air folk museum is opened.
1938	Germany forces Eduard Beneš to resign as president.
1939	Nazis occupy Bohemia and Moravia. World War II begins.

1945 World War II ends. The International Folklore Festival is established.

1948 Communist leader Klement Gottwald becomes president of Czechoslovakia, and the country develops stronger ties to the Soviet Union.

1960 The Communist government adopts a new constitution, and the country is renamed the Czechoslovak Socialist Republic.

1968 Alexander Dubcek introduces the Prague Spring.

1971 Musicians start the anti-Communist Jazz Federation.

1977 The human rights group Charter 77 is formed.

1984 Graphic designer Joska Skalnik invites artists to create box art.

1989 Pro-democracy demonstrations spark the Velvet Revolution.

1990 In free elections, the Communist regime is replaced by a democratic government.

1992 The Czech parliament adopts a new constitution.

1993 Slovakia gains independence; Bohemia and Moravia become the Czech Republic.

1998 The Czech Republic's hockey team wins an Olympic gold medal.

2000 The Czech Republic hosts Forum 2000, a conference promoting human rights, health and education for children, and environmental protection.

2002 The government votes to increase the minimum wage to combat unemployment. The worst flooding the country has experienced in 150 years causes severe damage to Prague and other areas.

COUNTRY NAME Czech Republic

AREA 30,448 square miles (78,864 sq. km)

MAIN LANDFORMS Bohemian Basin, Bohemian Forest, Bohemian-Moravian Highlands, Carpathian Mountains, Český Les Mountains, Jeseník Mountains, Krkonoše Mountains, Moravian Lowlands, Moravsky Kras, Ore Mountains, Šumava Mountains

HIGHEST POINT Mount Sněžka, 5,256 feet (1,602 m) above sea level

LOWEST POINT Labe River at Hrensko, 377 feet (115 m) above sea level

MAJOR RIVERS Berounka River, Dyje River, Labe River, Morava River, Odra River, Sazava River, Svratka River, Vltava River

ANIMALS alpine ibex, badgers, brown bears, chamois, deer, hedgehogs, lynx, marmots, martens, mouflons, otters, squirrels, wild boars, wolves

CAPITAL CITY Prague

OTHER MAJOR CITIES Brno, Ostrava, Plzeň, Olomouc

OFFICIAL LANGUAGE Czech

MONETARY UNIT Czech koruna. 100 hellers=1 koruna

CZECH CURRENCY

The Czech unit of money is the Czech koruna, or Czech crown, which was adopted February 8, 1993, and was equal in value to the former Czechoslovakia koruna. The koruna consists of 100 hellers, also known as hal. There are coins of 10, 20, and 50 hals, as well as coins of 1, 2, 5, 10, and 20 korunas. Bank notes include 20, 50, 100, 200, 500, 1,000, 2,000, and 5,000 korunas.

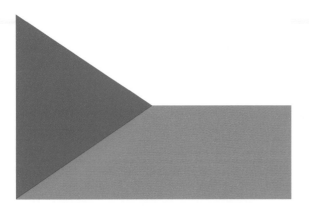

The state flag of the Czech Republic is similar to the flag adopted by Czechoslovakia in 1920. The flag's design consists of two equal horizontal bands—white on top and red on the bottom. A blue triangle lies with its base on the hoist side. When the Communists took control of the government, the flag was changed to two equal bands of white and red—the flag design of all former Soviet bloc countries. After Slovakia declared its independence in the 1990s, the Czech Republic restored the blue triangle to its flag.

Flag

The Czech Republic's national anthem, "Where Is My Home?," was created in 1834 by composer Frantisek Skroup and lyricist Josef Tyl. Known simply at the time as "Song Number 19," the song gained instant popularity. When the Czech people won their independence from Austria in 1918, they chose this favorite melody as their national song. While the anthem's melody has remained untouched, the words have been altered many times to reflect the country's situation. Below is an English translation of one of the anthem's verses.

National Anthem

"Where Is My Home?"

Where is my home, where is my home?
Water bubbles across the meadows,
Pinewoods rustle among crags,
The garden is glorious with spring blossom,
Paradise on earth it is to see.
And this is that beautiful land,
The Czech land, my home,
The Czech land, my home.

 For a link where you can listen to the Czech Republic's national anthem, "Where Is My Home?," go to vgsbooks.com.

ANTONÍN DVOŘÁK (1841–1904) Antonín Dvořák was a composer whose music was greatly influenced by local Bohemian folk melodies. Dvořák first gained recognition as a composer in 1873 with his cantata *Hymnus.* In 1878 his *Slavonic Dances* were published, making him instantly famous. His works soon brought him international fame, and he was invited to the National Conservatory in New York City, where he served as artistic director from 1892 to 1895. During this time, he wrote his most famous symphony, *From the New World.* Dvořák was born in Nelahozeves.

MILOŠ FORMAN (b. 1932) Born in Caslav, Miloš Forman has become an internationally renowned film director. His most famous works include *Amadeus, The People vs. Larry Flint,* and *Man on the Moon.* His most famous American work, *One Flew over the Cuckoo's Nest,* won all five major Academy Awards, including Best Picture and Best Director, in 1976. After the Communist regime took control of Czechoslovakia, Forman defected to the United States.

DOMINIK HASEK (b. 1965) Dominik Hasek is a professional hockey player who was born in Pardubice. As a world-class goalie, Hasek led the Czech Republic to Olympic gold during the 1998 games at Nagano, Japan. He played for the Buffalo Sabres from 1992 to 2000, and he won the National Hockey League's Most Valuable player in 1997 and 1998. Hasek began playing for the Detroit Red Wings in 2001.

VÁCLAV HAVEL (b. 1936) Born to a wealthy family in Prague, Václav Havel was a playwright and political dissident. In 1977 he cofounded the anti-Communist Charter 77 initiative. Havel was elected president of Czechoslovakia in 1989. After Slovakia declared its independence in 1993, he was elected as president of the newly formed Czech Republic. For his literary achievements and his human rights work, Havel has received numerous international awards.

FRANZ KAFKA (1883–1924) Franz Kafka was a writer born in Prague. While none of his writings was ever printed during his lifetime, he became one of the most influential writers of the twentieth century. A common theme in his works is the loneliness modern humans feel in a hostile world. His most famous works include *The Trial, Metamorphosis, The Castle,* and *Amerika.*

KAREL MÁCHA (1810–1836) Karel Mácha was a Czech poet who penned the epic poem *Maj (May),* considered the finest lyric work in the Czech language. His work is known for its melancholy and nostalgic feel and its powerful imagery. Mácha was born in Prague.

MARIA THERESA (1717–1780) Maria Theresa, who was born in Vienna, Austria, became Austrian empress and queen of Hungary and Bohemia in 1740. In 1745 she became empress of the Holy Roman Empire.

During her reign, she worked to reform the Hapsburg administration by centralizing power and bringing the Church under stricter state control. She implemented social reforms in the areas of justice, education, farming, and medicine.

ALFONS MUCHA (1860–1939)
A Czech painter and designer, Alfons Mucha was a leader in the art nouveau movement, a decorative style of asymmetrical lines and delicate human figures whose hair and clothing blend with the background in elaborate detail. His most famous works are poster designs featuring the French actress Sarah Bernhardt. Mucha was born in the Moravian town of Ivanèice.

MARTINA NAVRATILOVÁ (b. 1956)
Martina Navratilová is a tennis player who holds the women's all-time record for singles championships. Born in Prague, Navratilová was the national champion in her native country from 1972 to 1975. She defected to the United States in 1975. Her biography, *Martina,* was published in 1985, and she continued to rank as a top player until her retirement in 1994.

BOŽENA NEMCOVÁ (1820–1862)
Božena Nemcová was an author who remains the most famous female Czech writer. She wrote poetry, fairy tales, and short stories in addition to novels. A staunch nationalist, she drew on her rural Bohemian childhood for inspiration for her works. Her most popular book, *Grandmother,* was translated into more than one hundred languages. The story describes rural family life in Bohemia. Nemcova was born in the Bohemian countryside.

FRANTIŠEK PALACKÝ (1798–1876)
Born in Moravia, František Palacký was a Czech nationalist and historian. Due to his literary and political contributions to the Czech national revival in the early to mid-1800s, Palacký is often considered the father of the modern Czech nation. His historical works encouraged a renewed interest in Czech culture and literature. Palacký served as head of the first Pan-Slav Congress in 1848 and worked to achieve Czech independence.

PETER SÍS (b. 1949)
Peter Sís is an author, illustrator, and filmmaker who was born in Brno. He studied at the Academy of Applied Arts in Prague and in London. In 1984 Sís settled in New York City, where he began writing and illustrating children's books. His works include *Tibet: Through the Red Box, The Three Golden Keys, Komodo!,* and *A Small Tall Tale from the Far, Far North.* He has won numerous awards for his works.

BEDŘICH SMETANA (1824–1884)
Bedřich Smetana was Bohemia's first major nationalist composer. His music, operas, and symphonies drew on Bohemia's legends, history, and landscapes. Smetana's most famous works include his operas *The Bartered Bride, Dalibor,* and *Libuse,* and his symphonic poem *Má Vlast (My Country).* He was born in Litomysl.

CATHEDRAL OF SAINT BARTHOLOMEW Rising 333 feet (101 m), this Gothic cathedral in Plzeň boasts the tallest steeple in the Czech Republic. A marble Madonna stands at the main altar.

CESKY KRUMLOV Highlights of this historic Bohemian town include the Regional Museum, which houses artifacts from the town's colorful past, and the Česky Krumlov Château, the second largest castle in Bohemia.

CHARLES BRIDGE Built in the fourteenth century, Charles Bridge runs from Prague Castle to Stare Mesto (Old Town). Considered one of Prague's most important structures, the bridge draws many street musicians and artists to entertain pedestrians.

JOSEFOV Visitors to Josefov, the Old Jewish Quarter, can learn about Prague's Jewish past. Sights here include the Old Jewish Cemetery, the Old-New Synagogue, and the Jewish Museum.

KARLOVY VARY Discovered by Charles IV in the fourteenth century, Karlovy Vary has become world famous for its mineral waters and spas. Besides its springs, this town in Bohemia features various shops and cafés.

KUTNÁ HORA This medieval town near Prague was once the second most important city in Bohemia. Main attractions are Saint Barbara's Cathedral, Okreski Museum, and the Bone Church, which is filled with human bones arranged in sculptures.

MORAVIAN KARST This natural wonder near Brno features caverns and canyons carved by the underground Punkva River. Visitors can trek through the caves or take a boat ride on the Punkva.

MORAVSKE SLOVACKO This region is rich in folk art and festivals. Villagers in the various towns continue to use traditional Czech costumes, speech, and art and architectural styles.

NOVE MESTO (NEW TOWN) Prague's New Town is home to many monuments of the Czechs' rise to independence. Highlights here are Municipal House, Wenceslas Square, Vysehrad Castle, and the National Theater.

PRAGUE CASTLE Prague Castle, which dates to the ninth century, is actually a complex of houses, towers, churches, and courtyards. Popular sights here include Saint Vitus Cathedral, the Royal Palace, Saint George's Basilica, and the Golden Lane.

STARE MESTO (OLD TOWN) Prague's Old Town features some of the country's most famous sites, including Tyn Church, Smetana Museum, Church of Saint Nicholas, Old Town Square, and Estates Theatre.

acid rain: rain or snow that contains chemicals from pollutants such as coal smoke or vehicle exhaust

atheist: a person who does not believe in the existence of God or gods

Catholicism: a Christian religion based on the teachings of Jesus Christ and founded in the first century A.D. The pope, who is based in Vatican City in Italy, is the head of the Catholic Church.

communism: a theory of common ownership; a system of government in which the government controls industry and agriculture

defenestration: throwing someone or something out of a window

free-market system: an economic system in which supply and demand determine the cost of goods

Hussites: followers of the fourteenth century religious reformer Jan Hus, who believed the Catholic Church was corrupt. Hussites wanted to restore simpler teachings and customs to the Church.

nationalist: a person or group who feels supreme loyalty toward their nation and strongly emphasizes the promotion of a national culture and national interests, including independence

Prague Spring: the nickname for the period in the 1960s when Czech leader Alexander Dubcek allowed greater civil liberties than in other Communist countries

Protestant: any western Christian religion not affiliated with the Catholic Church

serfdom: a system in which peasants, or serfs, are required to render services to their lord, often in exchange for land or protection

Velvet Revolution: the 1989 peaceful protest that led to the fall of the Communist regime in Czechoslovakia

Glossary

Altman, Jack. *Prague*. Heathrow, FL: AAA Publishing, 2002.
This travel guide to Prague features information about the capital city's highlights and how to get around.

CountryWatch. 2002.
<http://www.countrywatch.com/cw_country.asp?vcountry=131> (June 2, 2002).
CountryWatch includes information about the Czech Republic including its political history, economic conditions, environmental issues, and social customs.

Czech.cz. N.d.
<http://www.czech.cz/> (June 7, 2002).
The official site of the Czech Republic's government offers information about living and working in the Czech Republic, as well as cultural and political history.

Demetz, Peter. *Prague in Black and Gold*. New York: Hill and Wang, 1997.
Demetz covers the history and highlights of this European city, including the legends of its origins, its colorful literary traditions, and its political past.

Europa Year World Book. Vol. 1. London: Europa Publications Ltd., 2001.
The article covering the Czech Republic includes recent events, vital statistics, and economic information.

Kirschbaum, Stanislav. *A History of Slovakia: The Struggle for Survival*. New York: St. Martin's Press, 1995.
This book covers the evolution of the Slovak nation from its earliest inhabitants to its declaration of independence in 1993, including its shared history with the Czech Republic.

Krejci, Jaroslav. *Czechoslovakia at the Crossroads of European History*. London: I. B. Taurus and Company, 1990.
Krejci discusses the historical framework and political climate of Czechoslovakia as factors in the country's shift from Communism to democracy.

Martin, Pat, comp. *Czechoslovak Culture: Recipes, History, and Folk Arts*. Iowa City, IA: Penfield Press, 1989.
Learn more about the culture of the Czech Republic through its food and folk arts.

Otfinoski, Steven. *The Czech Republic*. New York: Facts on File, 1997.
Otfinoski gives an in-depth look at the history, economy, and government of the Czech Republic. Highlights include the chapters on daily life and the nation's cities.

Population Reference Bureau. June 2, 2002.
<http://www.prb.org> (June 2, 2002).
The bureau offers current population figures, vital statistics, land area, and more. Special articles cover the latest environmental and health issues that concern each country, including the Czech Republic.

Selected Bibliography

Prihodova-Mastrini, Hana, and Alan Crosby. *Prague and the Best of the Czech Republic.* **4th edition. New York: Hungry Minds, Inc., 2002.**
This guide offers travel tips for getting around the Czech Republic as well as historical and cultural information.

Statesman's Yearbook. **London: Macmillan, 2001.**
This resource features information about the Czech Republic's historical events, industry and trade, climate and topography, as well as suggestions for further reading.

The World Factbook. **January 1, 2001.**
<http://www.cia.gov/cia/publications/factbook/geos/ez.html> (June 2, 2002).
This website features up-to-date information about the people, land, economy, and government of the Czech Republic. Transnational issues are also briefly covered.

World Gazetteer. **February 15, 2002.**
<http://www.gazetteer.de> (June 2, 2002).
The World Gazetteer offers population information about cities, towns, and places for the Czech Republic and other countries, including their administrative divisions.

Cather, Willa. *My Ántonia.* **New York: Modern Library, 1996.**
This novel tells the tale of a young girl born to Bohemian immigrants in Nebraska.

Czechia
<http://ling.osu.edu/~hana/Czechia.html>
This website includes fun facts, history, and famous people from the Czech Republic.

Hasek, Jaroslav. *The Good Soldier Svejk and His Fortunes in the World War.* **New York: Alfred A. Knopf, 1993.**
This satire follows the outrageous adventures of a Czech man drafted by the Austrian Army during World War I.

Havel, Václav. *Open Letters: Selected Writings, 1965–1990.* **New York: Knopf, 1990.**
This collection of essays, letters, and interviews covers the Czech Republic's most famous dissident as he goes from a playwright and political prisoner to president.

Haviland, Virginia. *Favorite Fairy Tales Told in Czechoslovakia.* **New York: Beech Tree Books, 1995.**
Learn more about Czech folk culture through such legends as the Wood Fairy and Kurkato the Terrible.

Kafka, Franz. *Collected Stories.* **New York: Alfred A. Knopf, 1993.**
This collection includes Kafka's most famous works, including *Metamorphosis*—the nightmarish tale of a man who wakes up to find himself transformed into a giant insect.

Kanefield, Teri. *Rivka's Way.* **Chicago: Cricket Books, 2001.**
Rivka, a fifteen-year-old Jewish girl living in Prague in 1778, dresses up as a boy to explore the city. During her outings, she meets a young man named Mikul, who must work to pay off his late mother's debts.

Nollen, Tim. *Culture Shock! Czech Republic.* **Portland, OR: Graphic Arts Center Publishing, 2002.**
Learn facts about daily life in the Czech Republic and tips for traveling there.

Press, Petra. *Czech Republic.* **San Diego, CA: Lucent Books, 2002.**
This book features a broad overview of the Czech Republic. History, geography, and fun facts are covered.

Radio Prague Online
<http://www.radio.cz/english>
This online version of Radio Prague covers current news events in the Czech Republic in English.

Sioras, Efstathia. *Czech Republic.* **New York: Marshall Cavendish, 1999.**
This book for younger readers includes chapters on the language, arts, and recreational activities of the Czech people.

Further Reading and Websites

Sís, Peter. *The Three Golden Keys.* **New York: Farrar, Straus and Giroux, 2001.**
A semiautobiographical picture book for all ages, this is the tale of a man returning to his childhood home, Prague. Text and illustrations take readers on a tour of Prague and introduce Czech fairy tales.

Symynkywicz, Jeffrey. *Václav Havel and the Velvet Revolution.* **Parsipanny, NJ: Dillon Press, 1995.**
This biography covers the life of one of the Czech Republic's greatest heroes.

vgsbooks.com
<http://www.vgsbooks.com>
Visit vgsbooks.com, the homepage of the Visual Geography Series®. You can get linked to all sorts of useful on-line information, including geographical, historical, demographic, cultural, and economic websites. The vgsbooks.com site is a great resource for late-breaking news and statistics.

Volavkova, Hana, ed. *I Never Saw Another Butterfly: Children's Drawings and Poems from Terezín Concentration Camp, 1942–1944.* **New York: Schocken Books, 1993.**
This collection gathers poems and drawings created by children imprisoned in the Nazi concentration camp near Terezín, Czechoslovakia, during World War II.

Captions for photos appearing on cover and chapter openers:

Cover: Sightseers stroll through Prague's Old Town Square.

pp. 4–5 The main square in the Czech town of Telc is lined with well-preserved buildings that date back to the sixteenth century.

pp. 8–9 The village of Kremesnik lies in a hilly area of the Czech Republic.

pp. 38–39 Crowds cross the Charles Bridge in Prague on a summer day.

pp. 46–47 Children dressed in traditional Moravian costumes perform a folk dance.

pp. 56–57 This steel mill is one of many factories in the industrial town of Kladno.

Photo Acknowledgments
The images in this book are used with the permission of: © A.A.M. Van der Heyden/Independent Picture Service, pp. 4–5; PresentationMaps.com, pp 6, 13; © M. Cerny/TRIP Photographic Library, pp. 8–9, 12; © Oldrich Karasek/Peter Arnold, Inc., pp. 10, 40, 43, 45, 46–47, 48; © Buddy Mays/TRAVELSTOCK, p. 11; © T. Bognar/TRIP Photographic Library, pp. 15, 22, 53; © C. Rennie/ TRIP Photographic Library, p. 16; © Jonathan Blair/CORBIS, p. 17; © Stock Montage/SuperStock, p. 20; © SuperStock, pp. 23, 38–39, 56–57; © Jaime Abecasis/SuperStock, p. 24; © A.K.G., Berlin/SuperStock, p. 25; © Museum of Art History, Vienna/A.K.G., Berlin/SuperStock, p. 26; © Bettmann/CORBIS, pp. 27, 33, 52; © Scheufler Collection/CORBIS, p. 28; © CORBIS, p. 29; © Independent Picture Service, pp. 30, 31, 32; © Peter Turnley/CORBIS, p. 34; © E. Parker/TRIP Photographic Library, p. 35; © Reuters NewMedia Inc./ CORBIS, p. 36; © Barry Lewis/CORBIS, p. 41; © B. Gibbs/TRIP Photographic Library, p. 42; © D. Harding/ TRIP Photographic Library, p. 50; © Dvorak Museum, Prague, Czechoslovakia/ ET Archive, London/SuperStock, p. 51; © Steve Ross/TRIP Photographic Library, p. 55; © Ask Images/TRIP Photographic Library, p. 59; © Dave G. Houser/CORBIS, p. 61; © A. Ghazzal/ TRIP Photographic Library, p. 62; © N. & J. Wiseman/TRIP Photographic Library, p. 63; © Wolfgang Kaehler, p. 64; © Todd Strand/Independent Picture Service, p. 68; Laura Westlund, p. 69.

Cover photo: © R. Westlake/TRIP Photographic Library. Back cover photo: NASA.